W9-BWJ-095

"This book consolidates Stephanie Moulton Sarkis's expertise and experience into a 'first step' guide for those diagnosed as an adult with attention deficit/hyperactivity disorder (ADHD). An important contribution for ADHD adults, this book is easy to read, with concise sections that allow readers to quickly grasp important information. This book is an excellent starting point for newly diagnosed adults with ADHD and family members hoping to understand the disorder."

> —David W. Goodman, MD, assistant professor at Johns Hopkins School of Medicine and director at Adult Attention Deficit Disorder Center of Maryland

"While there have been several good adult ADHD introductory books, Sarkis's new guide provides updated value in a rapidly advancing field. In addition to explaining just what to do, she skillfully advises about how to work through the process, highlighting the importance of ongoing personal and professional helping relationships."

> —Richard L. Rubin, MD, vice president of the American Professional Society for ADHD and Related Disorders and adjunct associate professor of Dartmouth Medical College

"If you've just been diagnosed with ADD, you need this book. It will guide you step by step through understanding the diagnosis and the best treatments for you. This book will help you find hope and figure out your next steps."

> —Lara Honos-Webb, Ph.D., author of *The Gift of Adult ADD*

"The first and most important thing the newly diagnosed can do is to educate themselves about ADHD. But where to begin? In a thoroughly accessible and practical way, Sarkis covers all the major topics. This is a great first book to read after being diagnosed with ADHD because it gives you the lay of the land and guides you toward the topics you may want to learn more about."

—Ari Tuckman, Psy.D., MBA, author of *More Attention, Less Deficit* and *Integrative Treatment for Adult ADHD*

Adult
ADD

A GUIDE *for* THE NEWLY DIAGNOSED

Stephanie Moulton Sarkis, Ph.D.

New Harbinger Publications, Inc.

Publisher's Note

Care has been taken to confirm the accuracy of the information presented and to describe generally accepted practices. However, the authors, editors, and publisher are not responsible for errors or omissions or for any consequences from application of the information in this book and make no warranty, express or implied, with respect to the contents of the publication.

The authors, editors, and publisher have exerted every effort to ensure that any drug selection and dosage set forth in this text are in accordance with current recommendations and practice at the time of publication. However, in view of ongoing research, changes in government regulations, and the constant flow of information relating to drug therapy and drug reactions, the reader is urged to check the package insert for each drug and consult with their health care provider for any change in indications and dosage and for added warnings and precautions. This is particularly important when the recommended agent is a new or infrequently employed drug.

Some drugs and medical devices presented in this publication may have Food and Drug Administration (FDA) clearance for limited use in restricted research settings. It is the responsibility of the health care provider to ascertain the FDA status of each drug or device planned for use in their clinical practice.

Distributed in Canada by Raincoast Books

Copyright © 2011 by Stephanie Sarkis
New Harbinger Publications, Inc.
5674 Shattuck Avenue
Oakland, CA 94609
www.newharbinger.com

Cover design by Amy Shoup; Text design by Michele Waters-Kermes; Acquired by Melissa Kirk; Edited by Elisabeth Beller

All Rights Reserved. Printed in Canada.

Library of Congress Cataloging-in-Publication Data

Sarkis, Stephanie.
  Adult ADD : a guide for the newly diagnosed / Stephanie Moulton Sarkis ; foreword by Patricia O. Quinn.
    p. cm.
  Includes bibliographical references.
  ISBN 978-1-60882-005-4 (pbk.) -- ISBN 978-1-60882-006-1 (pdf ebook) 1. Attention-deficit disorder in adults--Popular works. 2. Attention-deficit disorder in adults--Treatment--Popular works. 3. Self-care, Health. I. Title.

RC394.A85S264 2011
616.85'89--dc22

                                  2010046099

This book is printed with soy ink.

13   12   11

10   9   8   7   6   5   4   3   2   1   First printing

FSC
Mixed Sources
Product group from well-managed forests, controlled sources and recycled wood or fiber
Cert no. SW-COC-000952
www.fsc.org
© 1996 Forest Stewardship Council

This book is dedicated to everyone who is beginning a journey with ADD and to everyone who has been taking the journey for a while and has just discovered a new guidebook.

CONTENTS

	Foreword	vii
	Acknowledgments	xi
	Introduction	1
CHAPTER 1	Overview of ADD	5
CHAPTER 2	Finding a Treatment Team	18
CHAPTER 3	Diagnosis	31
CHAPTER 4	Treatments for ADD	54
CHAPTER 5	Additional Concerns When You Have ADD	74
CHAPTER 6	Lifestyle Changes	87
CHAPTER 7	Getting Support	98
CHAPTER 8	ADD and the Workplace	108
CHAPTER 9	The Positives of Having ADD	118
	Conclusion	128
	Resources	129
	Recommended Reading	133
	References	135

Foreword

Congratulations! You've just found out that you have ADD…
and…you're reading this book—two important steps on the
path to transforming your future into one with fewer struggles
and greater happiness and success. Now you might be thinking,
"How can having ADD possibly be a good thing?" Well, I can
assure you that finding the answer to why your life has been so
difficult to date can change everything.

Attention deficit disorder (ADD) is a hopeful diagnosis.
Today, there are many professionals, including physicians, therapists, coaches, professional organizers, and educators, all dedicated to working with you to develop new skills and a plan for
success. There are also many new medical breakthroughs and
longer-acting medications to treat the symptoms of ADD that

have proven to be both extremely safe and effective. In addition, you'll find books like *Adult ADD: A Guide for the Newly Diagnosed* as well as websites that contain a great deal of information and many useful techniques and strategies to control clutter, organize your schedule, and even find a new career, if that's what you are looking for.

With all this knowledge comes power—the power to take control of your life and rewrite your story. Over the thirty-some-odd years that I have been a practicing physician specializing in the diagnosis and treatment of ADD, I've worked with many adults and seen some amazing transformations. I remember receiving an e-mail from a middle-aged woman who confided that after her diagnosis she had begun taking medication and seen remarkable changes in her ability to stay on track and complete projects. She also confessed that she had recently dyed her hair red. I must admit I was puzzled and felt that perhaps her medication dosage was not correct and that she was still acting impulsively. However, upon further reading, I saw that she had gone on to say that she was tired of being thought of as a "dumb blonde" and wanted a new image. Then there was the man from Massachusetts who called looking for help after he had just lost his twenty-second job, but who, upon receiving a diagnosis of ADD, was able to work with a therapist to deal with both his depression and other self-destructive habits and behaviors. When I contacted him three years later to follow up and see how he was doing, he proudly proclaimed that he had started his own small business, which was still going strong and providing him with a good income and a deep sense of personal satisfaction.

Now don't get me wrong. I'm not saying that ADD is a gift. The disorder most certainly comes with difficulties and many behaviors that are not only problematic for you but frustrating for others in your life as well. And untreated ADD can certainly limit your potential. Knowing you have ADD, however, is an explanation for why things have been so difficult. It is *not* an excuse for slacking off, giving up, or settling for less. An explanation helps you understand and give meaning to your behaviors. It does not define who you are or limit your potential. An excuse, however, limits you and what you can or are willing to do. It makes you less. ADD should never be an excuse for bad behavior or poor performance.

Adults with ADD are often their own harshest critics. Their life experiences only confirm for them their sense of failure to live up to the expectations they have set for themselves or others have set for them. When you put a label on what you are experiencing, you open the door to change. By viewing your problems and failures through the lens of a real neurobiological disorder and seeing these issues in the larger context of strengths and weaknesses instead of blaming yourself, you often gain a sense of relief. Instead of perceiving your problems as unchangeable, you finally can accept who you are and exchange hopelessness for hope and criticism for compassion.

Through education and a total treatment program, you can create for yourself a more ADD-friendly lifestyle. An ADD-friendly lifestyle is one in which you draw on your strengths and let them carry you through your weaknesses. Living an ADD-friendly lifestyle allows you to forgive past mistakes and use humor to get through your present trials as you work with your

ADD instead of always fighting against it. It allows you to set in motion a program to meet your unique needs and to become more productive.

In the end, keep in mind that ADD is only a part of who you are. Don't be defined by your disability. Don't be the one to say you can't, and don't let your past define your future! Do believe that you are more than your ADD and act as if you can be successful and happy. And above all...do let the future become the now and live your dream!

Patricia O. Quinn, MD
Director, National Center for
Girls and Women with ADHD
Washington, DC

ACKNOWLEDGMENTS

Thank you to my patients and clients, from whom I have learned so much. Thank you to my editors at New Harbinger: Melissa Kirk, Jess Beebe, and Elisabeth Beller. Thank you also to Jesse Burson, Earlita Chenault, Adia Colar, and Julia Kent at New Harbinger. Thank you to Patricia O. Quinn, MD; Kelly Aissen, Ph.D.; Lori Burack, LCSW; Charles Downer, Ph.D.; Lara Honos-Webb, Ph.D.; Stephanie Hunter-Banks, Pharm.D.; Irene Kerzhnerman, Ph.D.; Jane Marinelli, ARNP; Roberto Olivardia, Ph.D.; Nancy Ratey, M.Ed.; Richard Rubin, MD; Elias Sarkis, MD; Ari Tuckman, Psy.D., and Sharon Wigal, Ph.D. for their help and contributions. Thank you also to William Moulton, Janice Moulton, Claude Moulton, Christine Whitney, Charles

Gates Kmet, Eric Rogell, Katie Degnan, Denise Gauthier, Paul Gauthier, Toby Sarkis, and Lucy Sarkis for their support.

INTRODUCTION

Does this sound like you? Your whole life you've had difficulty getting your work done, getting to appointments on time,
keeping up friendships, and listening more than talking—and
now you know why. You've just been diagnosed with attention
deficit disorder (ADD). Finally, all the puzzle pieces fit. Now
you know why you get bored almost instantly. Now you know
why you've jumped from job to job or relationship to relationship trying to figure out why none of them "clicked" for you. But
wait—your journey has just begun.

There may be a bunch of questions running through your
mind now that you've been diagnosed with ADD: What now?
What's the next step? Whom should you tell about your diagnosis, and how do you tell them about it? What treatment options

are available? What emotions will you be going through during this process? Whom should you turn to for support? This book will answer those questions and more. Consider it your road map through the new territory of ADD. The journey can be challenging but also fulfilling. In the following chapters, you will learn how to live your life to the fullest, even if you tend to be impulsive and distracted.

In chapter 1, you will learn about the symptoms, the diagnostic criteria, and the subtypes of ADD. You will discover more about how ADD affects your quality of life and how ADD symptoms change from childhood to adulthood. You will learn the biological and genetic causes of ADD. You will find out about the roles of dopamine and the "executive functions" of the brain and how they affect ADD.

In chapter 2, you will find out how to put together your treatment team—a group of clinicians and other professionals who can help you with ADD diagnosis and treatment. This team includes psychiatrists, psychologists, counselors, and coaches. You will learn about the different roles of each of these professionals and how to find a doctor who is a good fit for you.

In chapter 3, you will learn the process of ADD diagnosis. You will find out how your first meeting (or evaluation) with your doctor might go, the information you might be asked for, and what paperwork to bring with you. You will also learn about the tests, questionnaires, and forms that your doctor might want you to fill out as well as the pros and cons of filing for reimbursement with your medical insurance company. You will also learn about the feelings you may go through after you've been diagnosed with ADD.

In chapter 4, you will learn about the treatment options available for ADD and their effectiveness. Treatment options include medication, counseling, coaching, and neurofeedback. The chapter provides information about the different types of medications that are prescribed for ADD. You will also discover the differences between counseling and coaching.

In chapter 5, you will learn about the different concerns, such as substance abuse, depression, anxiety, and eating disorders, that can come up more frequently when you have ADD. You will learn the symptoms, how to know if you need help, and how to get help for each of these problems.

In chapter 6, you will gain information about lifestyle changes that can make things easier for you when you have ADD. Changes include reducing clutter and taking better care of yourself. You'll learn a simple and manageable way to keep your home or office organized. You'll get information on taking care of yourself physically and emotionally—by eating appropriately, getting enough exercise, and sleeping well.

In chapter 7, you will learn about getting support from the different people in your life—your spouse or partner, children, other family, and friends. You will discover how to talk to your family and friends about ADD. You will also be provided with the pros and cons of different types of support groups, including online support.

In chapter 8, you will learn about accommodations that can make your workday easier and more productive. You will also learn the pros and cons of disclosing your ADD diagnosis to your employer. You will discover characteristics of those jobs in which people with ADD excel.

After reading about the challenges of ADD, it is good to discover the positive traits you have as well. In chapter 9, you'll learn how people with ADD tend to be more creative and "think outside the box" and how to use your abilities and talents to improve your community and the world around you.

Throughout these chapters, you will hear from people just like you who are experiencing, coping with, and living successfully with ADD. You will also hear from professionals who specialize in ADD. At the end of the book, you will find information on resources that will help further expand your knowledge of ADD. Good luck on your new journey!

CHAPTER 1

OVERVIEW OF ADD

Since you've been diagnosed with ADD, you may remember even more that you always felt like you didn't fit in. You may have felt this way even from the time you were a small child. You always seemed to be one or two steps behind everyone else. In grade school you never turned your work in on time. When you opened your desk, papers would come flying out. Your report cards had teacher comments such as "doesn't work to potential" or "talks out of turn." When you played games with your friends, you would forget whose turn it was next. You would interrupt your friends and act way sillier than they did—which led to you losing friends.

As you got older, you continued to struggle through school and found yourself skipping classes and maybe even dropping out. People still tell you that you aren't working to your potential. You've had a string of failed relationships, mainly due to your impulsive spending and difficulties staying monogamous. You drink more than you should, because it helps your brain slow down and it helps you feel more comfortable in social situations. You also have gotten quite a few speeding tickets and may have even had your license suspended because you forgot to pay the fines. Does this sound familiar? You aren't the only one who has experienced issues like these. In the rest of this chapter, you will learn more about attention deficit disorder and how it affects your life and the lives of millions of others just like you.

WHAT IS ADD?

Attention deficit disorder (ADD) is a genetic and biological disorder that affects 4.4 percent of the U.S. population (Kessler et al. 2005). ADD is passed on through the genes you inherit from your parents. If you have ADD, there is a 75 percent chance that you inherited ADD genes from at least one of your parents (Rietveld et al. 2004).

There is nothing you did (or didn't do) to "get" ADD. You were born with the genes for it. Likewise, if your child has ADD, there is nothing you did to "cause" it. (Interestingly, many adults find out they have ADD after their children have been diagnosed with it. They realize their child's behavior is eerily similar to theirs when they were young.)

Scientists have identified several genes that are associated with ADD (Guan et al. 2009). There are also hundreds of gene variations that have been found in children who have ADD. These gene variations are not found in other children (Elia et al. 2010). Considering the recent advances in science, it is expected that more ADD-related genes and gene variations will be identified every year.

Although some people may doubt the validity of ADD, it is a serious and very real disorder. Adults with ADD have a significantly lower socioeconomic status, a lower level of academic achievement, and higher medical costs than their non-ADD peers (Kleinman et al. 2009; Bernfort, Nordfeldt, and Persson 2008). Adults with ADD also engage in more high-risk behaviors (such as gambling), have a higher rate of substance abuse, and have more car accidents (Breyer et al. 2009; Wilens and Upadhyaya 2007). They also have a higher rate of unplanned pregnancies and sexually transmitted diseases compared to people without ADD (Flory et al. 2006; Barkley et al. 2005).

Adults with ADD are also more likely to be unemployed. One study found that only 24 percent of ADD adults were employed, compared to 79 percent of non-ADD adults. This rate of employment improved with treatment for ADD symptoms (Halmey et al. 2009).

ADD Terms and Types

You have probably heard the terms "ADD" and "ADHD" both used to describe a pattern of inattention and impulsivity. The proper clinical term is "attention deficit hyperactivity disorder" (ADHD) even if you are just inattentive and not hyperactive. However, the term "ADD" is more frequently used by the general public. Therefore, in the remainder of the book, I will use the term "ADD."

The guide or book that lists the "official" symptoms of ADD is called the *Diagnostic and Statistical Manual of Mental Disorders* (DSM). This manual is published by the American Psychiatric Association and is the "gold standard" that clinicians use when diagnosing ADD. In the most recent version of the DSM, the *DSM-IV-TR* (APA [American Psychiatric Association] 2000), the term "ADHD" is used. The symptoms and other diagnostic criteria have, like the title of the disorder, changed over the years. (You will learn more about the history of ADD later in this chapter.)

According to the current diagnostic criteria, there are three subtypes of ADD: inattentive, hyperactive/impulsive, and combined (APA 2000).

SYMPTOMS OF THE INATTENTIVE SUBTYPE

To meet the criteria for the *inattentive subtype* of ADD, you must have at least six out of nine inattention symptoms:

- Distractibility

- Disorganization

- Difficulty paying attention to detail; making careless mistakes

- Forgetfulness

- Difficulty focusing or paying attention during tasks

- Difficulty following through on instructions and failing to finish tasks

- Avoiding tasks that require sustained mental effort

- Losing items often

- Not appearing to listen when spoken to

SYMPTOMS OF THE HYPERACTIVE/ IMPULSIVE SUBTYPE

To meet the criteria for the *hyperactive/impulsive subtype*, you must have at least six out of nine hyperactive/impulsive symptoms:

- A feeling of being "on the go" or acting as if "driven by a motor"

- Fidgetiness or squirming in seat

- Difficulty waiting turns or standing in line

- Interrupting or intruding on others

- Leaving seat when remaining seated is expected

- Blurting out answers before questions are completed

- Difficulty playing or engaging in leisure activities quietly

- Talking excessively

- Running around or climbing excessively

SYMPTOMS OF THE COMBINED SUBTYPE

If you meet at least six out of nine symptoms for the inattentive subtype and at least six out of nine symptoms for the hyperactive/impulsive subtype, then you meet the criteria for the *combined subtype* of ADD.

ADDITIONAL DIAGNOSTIC CRITERIA

The diagnostic criteria for ADD states that you must also have *impairment* as a result of these symptoms. This means that the symptoms of ADD that you do have must make a significant difference to your quality of life. You must also have difficulty with these symptoms in at least two of the following settings: home, school/work, and social settings.

In addition, according to diagnostic criteria, ADD symptoms must have been present before the age of seven. However, if you or your family members do not remember you having any hyperactive or inattentive behaviors before the age of seven, you may still meet all the criteria for the disorder. A study by Kieling and colleagues (2010) found that only 50 percent of ADD adults remembered having symptoms before the age of seven, but 99 percent reported having symptoms by the time they were sixteen years old.

It is normal for adults with ADD to have difficulty remembering events from their childhood. You are already more prone to distraction, so how are you supposed to remember what you did in the first grade? Your only childhood memories may be of traumatic events, such as having a bad bicycle accident or being ridiculed in front of your class in elementary school. You may also remember exciting events, such as your birthday parties or the first time you rode a bike without training wheels.

For the events that you do remember, ask yourself if those memories could be related to impulsive or distracted behavior. Also ask family members for their recollection of what you were like as a child. Since ADD is genetic, don't be surprised if your family members have difficulty remembering your childhood as well!

Causes and History of ADD

As you read earlier in the chapter, ADD is a genetic and biological disorder. However, the idea still persists that somehow people do something to cause ADD or that they are just "lazy." However, the fact that ADD is a genetic and biological disorder is gaining more credibility and proof, especially with improved medical technology. ADD is caused by a variety of biological factors, including difficulties with the executive functions of the brain and low dopamine levels. Next you will learn more about these biological differences in the ADD brain.

What we now know as "ADD" was once referred to as a "defect of moral control" (Still 1902). It was later referred to as *minimal brain dysfunction* because children had symptoms of impulsivity and hyperactivity without having any signs of brain injury or brain damage. In the 1950s, the condition became known as *hyperkinetic impulse disorder*. In the 1960s, the term changed to *hyperactive child syndrome*, and in the DSM-II (APA 1968), it was known as *hyperkinetic reaction of childhood*. In the DSM-III (APA 1980), it was called *attention-deficit disorder* to reflect the fact that the symptoms weren't just a result of the brain's "reaction" to something, as implied in the previous name. This is also when subtypes first made an appearance: with hyperactivity and without hyperactivity. Then, in the DSM-III-R (APA 1987), the disorder became known as *attention-deficit/ hyperactivity disorder*. Beginning with the DSM-IV (APA 1994), the name for the disorder is now *attention deficit hyperactivity disorder*.

You may be wondering why you are reading about the history of ADD. It is important to be aware that the symptoms of ADD have been around for a long time, even though the actual title of "ADD" is relatively recent. Through time, the name changed to reflect the increasing evidence that ADD is a biological disorder. Someone doesn't "choose" to be ADD or "catch" it through improper parenting—it is something that people are born with.

ADD IN ADULTS

You do not "grow out of" ADD, as once was commonly believed. Approximately 50 percent of children with ADD retain symptoms into adulthood (Wilens 2004). You may have noticed while looking at the ADD symptoms above that a lot of them apply to the behaviors of children. When you get older, your ADD symptoms change. You are probably less impulsive than when you were a child. This is because although your brain matures with age, it never really functions in the same way as a brain without ADD (McAlonan et al. 2009).

Symptoms of Adult ADD

Here are some symptoms that are not part of the DSM-IV-TR criteria but happen more frequently to adults with ADD:

- Putting too many activities on your schedule

- Making a lot of "to do" lists and never using them

- Getting multiple speeding tickets

- Having feelings of not living up to your potential

- Chronically procrastinating

- Angering quickly

- Having a feeling of inner restlessness

- Having difficulty making and keeping friends

- Having difficulty managing money

- Having low self-esteem

- Disliking traffic so much that you will drive out of your way to avoid it

- Interrupting people

- Being fired from multiple jobs

- Changing jobs frequently

- Being reprimanded at work for "carelessness" or for not following rules

- Having difficulty knowing the "unwritten" rules of the workplace

- Talking louder than others in social settings

Most people will have some of these symptoms at one point or another during their lives. The difference is that people with ADD experience these symptoms more frequently, more intensely, and for a longer period of time (or duration) than people without ADD. Also, when people with ADD have these symptoms, they cause impairment in their lives. As you can see, ADD doesn't just affect work life and school performance—it can also have detrimental effects on home life and social life.

Executive Functions of the Brain

People with ADD have difficulties with brain processes called *executive functions*. Executive functions are carried out by the brain's frontal lobes and include tasks such as processing information, initiating tasks, regulating moods, planning future behavior, and learning from consequences (Brown 2009; Barkley 2005). This means that people with ADD have difficulty getting motivated enough to start and follow through with tasks, they get frustrated more easily, and they just don't seem to learn from their mistakes.

You may have been told in the past, "You're smart. Why can't you can't finish this project (show up on time, learn from your mistakes)?" However, even ADD adults with high IQs have significantly more executive function difficulties than adults without ADD (Antshel et al. 2010).

There are also biological differences in the brains of people with ADD (Yacubian and Buchel 2009). In children with ADD, there is a disconnect between the frontal cortex of the brain, which regulates attention, and the visual processing areas of the brain. This difference does not occur in non-ADD children. This means that the way the brain pays attention is biologically different in those with ADD (Mazaheri et al. 2010).

Motivation

ADD isn't so much a problem with attention as it is a problem with motivation. The ADD brain doesn't get as jazzed by rewards as a non-ADD brain. Your brain just can't get motivated to follow through or finish tasks—nor can it be motivated to "switch gears" out of something it finds interesting. This may at least partially be because the ADD brain has a low amount of a *neurotransmitter* called dopamine (Volkow et al. 2009). Neurotransmitters are chemicals in the brain that signal from one *neuron*, or nerve cell, to another. It is how neurons communicate with each other. If there is difficulty with the communication between neurons, the brain doesn't work effectively. This means that the reward and motivation centers in the brain are not getting as much stimulation as they should, leading to inattention and hyperactivity. Brain scans even show that there is reduced activity in the motivation centers of the ADD brain, as compared to the non-ADD brain, during tasks.

When you have a low level of dopamine, your brain will try to find a way to raise it to "normal" levels. Activities that raise your brain's dopamine level include engaging in reckless or impulsive behaviors, such as illegal drug use. In chapter 5, you will learn more about these issues and increased risks that can go along with having a diagnosis of ADD. There is a regulated way of raising your dopamine—by taking ADD medication as prescribed. You will learn more about medication in chapter 4.

SUMMARY

In this chapter, you discovered that adults and children may not express ADD symptoms in the same way. You also learned that ADD is a genetic and biological disorder—it affects the way the brain's neurons communicate and how information is processed. You learned about the executive functions of the brain and how having difficulties with these functions can result in impulsivity and distraction. You learned that ADD is really a problem with motivation—which may, in part, be due to low levels of the neurotransmitter dopamine in the brain.

It is important to remember that everyone on this planet inherits something—if not genes for ADD, then genes for diabetes or heart disease or a variety of other disorders. Your "thing" just happens to be ADD. The good news is that there are professionals available who specialize in treating ADD. In chapter 2, you will learn how to find physicians, counselors, and other professionals who can best help you with your new journey through ADD territory.

CHAPTER 2

————————————————————————

FINDING A
TREATMENT TEAM

You've probably already been diagnosed with ADD, but whether you already have a diagnosis or are seeking an evaluation, it helps to have a team of mental health clinicians on your side. In this chapter, you will learn about the concept of a treatment team and the different types of clinicians who treat ADD. You will find out how to get a referral or recommendation for a clinician who specializes in ADD, do research before making an appointment, make an appointment, and make a decision about whether to include that person on your team.

WHAT IS A TREATMENT TEAM?

A *treatment team* is a group of clinicians who help you with your ADD diagnosis and treatment. They include clinicians who prescribe medication, conduct evaluations and testing, and do talk therapy (counseling). While you may be considering treating your ADD with medication only or with counseling alone, you may want to consider trying a combination of the two. Research shows that the most effective treatment may be a combination of medication and therapy (Jensen 2009; Weiss et al. 2008). You will learn more about ADD treatment options in chapter 4.

Prescribing Clinicians

There are different types of clinicians who can prescribe medication for ADD: psychiatrists, primary care physicians, advanced registered nurse practitioners, and physician's assistants. These clinicians are described below and are listed in order from the most to the least medical training received. All of the following clinicians can be found in each of the fifty states and in the District of Columbia.

PSYCHIATRISTS

Psychiatrists have graduated from medical school, have completed an internship and a residency, and have acquired additional training in mental health issues. They are the most qualified of the clinicians in terms of psychiatric knowledge and years of training. While psychiatrists in the past mainly did talk therapy or counseling, they are now more likely to prescribe medication. This is partially because there are many other types of clinicians who specialize in talk therapy but cannot prescribe medication. However, some psychiatrists may still see patients for a combination of medication treatment and talk therapy.

PRIMARY CARE PHYSICIANS

A primary care physician (PCP) is usually the "front line" person you see when you have any medical concerns. PCPs have completed medical school, an internship, a residency, and additional hours of training. A patient may be more likely to see a PCP than a specialist for mental health issues, due to the stigma that some may feel is attached to seeing a mental health clinician.

Your PCP may refer you to a psychiatrist or other mental health clinician for ADD diagnosis and treatment or may be comfortable prescribing the medication for you. While finding a specialist in ADD is recommended, there are certainly many PCPs who have educated themselves about ADD and other mental health conditions.

ADVANCED REGISTERED NURSE PRACTITIONERS

Advanced registered nurse practitioners (ARNPs) are nurses with additional education and years of training. ARNPs have at least a master's degree. They have training in psychiatry, and some have also elected to complete a certification in adult psychiatry. Nurse practitioners can prescribe all psychiatric medications, but they do need a physician to cosign prescriptions they write for stimulant medication. You will learn more about stimulant medication in chapter 4.

PHYSICIAN'S ASSISTANTS

Physician's assistants (PAs) are required to have at least a bachelor's degree. However, most PA programs now require a minimum of a master's degree. PAs also complete additional hours of training. They can write prescriptions for psychiatric medications, but all the prescriptions must be cosigned by a physician.

Nonprescribing Clinicians

There are other clinicians who specialize in ADD, conduct evaluations for ADD, do testing, and also can help you through talk therapy or counseling. Nonprescribing clinicians include psychologists and licensed professional counselors, clinical social workers, and marriage and family therapists. Many people with ADD also have issues with anxiety and depression. Talking about those issues, and learning new coping skills, may help you live a happier and more productive life. All of the following clinicians can be found in all fifty states and the District of Columbia.

PSYCHOLOGISTS

Psychologists must have a doctorate (Ph.D.) and have completed additional training. Psychologists do not prescribe medication, except in New Mexico, where they can prescribe psychiatric medications only after receiving appropriate training. There are different types of psychologists, such as counseling psychologists, clinical psychologists, and neuropsychologists. Your clinician may refer you to a neuropsychologist for evaluation and testing to help determine a diagnosis. You will learn more about evaluations and testing in chapter 3.

LICENSED PROFESSIONAL COUNSELORS

Licensed professional counselors (LPCs) or licensed mental health counselors (LMHCs) have at least a master's degree and have additional hours of training past graduation. Counselors can do evaluations, testing, and talk therapy.

LICENSED CLINICAL SOCIAL WORKERS

Licensed clinical social workers (LCSWs) have at least a master's degree and have completed additional hours of training. They are able to do evaluations, testing, and talk therapy. LCSWs tend to have more training in social services than other clinicians.

LICENSED MARRIAGE AND FAMILY THERAPISTS

Licensed marriage and family therapists (LMFTs) have at least a master's degree. They also have additional training in techniques and therapies that can help you get along better with your family and in your romantic relationship. This type of talk therapy or counseling is especially important for couples and families in which one or more people are affected by ADD. There tend to be more conflicts in ADD families than in non-ADD families due to the frustration, difficulties, and impulsivity caused by ADD.

HOW TO FIND AN ADD SPECIALIST

Remember, just because a clinician specializes in ADD does not necessarily make that clinician the best one for you. A clinician with whom you have a "good fit" is one who listens to your concerns, answers your questions to the best of his ability, has respect for your rights as a patient, gives you his recommendations, and tells you his concerns. First, however, you need to find a clinician who specializes in ADD.

If you know a friend or family member with ADD, you can ask whom he or she sees for treatment. Even if that clinician doesn't live in your city, you can contact him to ask whom he recommends in your area. You can also ask your PCP for a referral, or you may even find out that your PCP has additional training in ADD.

For more information on referrals or recommendations, visit ADD support groups, such as Children and Adults with Attention Deficit/Hyperactivity Disorder (CHADD) and the Attention Deficit Disorder Association (ADDA). There may be a CHADD or ADDA support group in your area where you can get information about referrals and possibly even meet clinicians who specialize in ADD. You may also find information on referrals or recommendations in online forums such as Attention Deficit Hyperactivity Disorder Forums. Contact information for CHADD, ADDA, and the forums can be found in Resources at the end of this book.

It wasn't until I turned forty that I was diagnosed with ADD. When I suspected I needed help—after a little Internet research—the first thing I did was look for a psychiatrist. The local universities were too busy, but one referred me to a psychiatrist who had experience with adult ADD. The psychiatrist diagnosed me with ADD using the DSM criteria, but he also sent me to a neuropsychologist for testing to confirm the diagnosis.

—Terry

CHOOSING AN ADD SPECIALIST

If you are filing a medical insurance claim and want to choose a clinician from your insurance company's network of providers, be aware that an ADD specialist in your area may not be within your insurer's network. You may want to consider paying extra in order to see an out-of-network provider. See chapter 3 for issues related to your privacy when you file a medical insurance claim.

Do Your Research

Before you call to make an appointment with a clinician to whom you have received a referral, do a little sleuthing on the Internet. Many states have clinicians' licenses in a searchable online database. The database will list if a clinician's license is up to date and if she has received any disciplinary action from the licensing board. You can also look up the clinician on an Internet search engine. You may find articles the clinician has written, awards she has received, and websites that list her as a clinician. You can even use the search term "ADD" along with the clinician's name to see what, specifically, she has done in the field.

The Advantages of a Group Practice

Some clinicians' offices, called *group practices*, have psychiatrists, psychologists, ARNPs, LPCs, and LCSWs working in the same office. There are even clinics where all the clinicians in the office specialize in ADD. One of the advantages to a group practice is that if you see more than one clinician at the office, your records are centrally located at the office. In addition, if you sign a medical release allowing your clinicians to speak to one another, it is much more efficient if your clinicians work in the same office. In addition, clinicians in the same office usually have an established working relationship and can communicate more effectively about your care than can clinicians who don't know each other. If you do see two clinicians at the same office, keep in mind that most medical insurance companies will not reimburse you for seeing a prescriber and a counselor on the same day.

Calling to Make an Appointment with a Clinician

Once you have received a recommendation or referral and have done your research, it is time to call the clinician's office for an appointment. When you call the office, tell them you are seeking a new-patient appointment. You can also tell them that you suspect you have ADD. It is up to you if you want to disclose any additional information. However, the more information you give, the more the staff can help you. The office staff may want to send you paperwork or may ask for your insurance information over the phone. (See chapter 3 for information on your privacy and filing with your medical insurer.) An exception to the rule of calling a clinician's office to make an appointment is if your medical insurance policy requires that you get a referral and an appointment through your primary care physician. See your insurance policy for more information.

When you call a clinician's office to make an appointment, you may find that the first available appointment is two, three, or even six months away. To get an earlier appointment, ask the staff if they have a *cancellation waitlist*. This means that if a patient cancels, you can be called to take the appointment time. This means that you might have to come in on short notice, but if you can do so, it can make the difference between waiting for an appointment a couple of months from now and being seen in a couple of weeks.

The office staff may tell you that although the clinician is no longer taking new patients, another clinician in the office (such as a psychiatrist, an ARNP, or a psychologist) can see you.

You may want to ask the following about the clinician:

- What training does the clinician have in ADD?

- How long has she been in practice?

- How long has she been treating ADD?

- What is the clinician's view on medications?

- Does she prescribe medications for ADD?

Know Your Patient Rights

When you attend an appointment with a doctor, you have certain patient rights. Your rights include:

- Viewing your chart and having a copy of your records

- Having your medical information kept confidential, with some legal exceptions

- Being treated with respect

- Being informed of your treatment options

- Making decisions about your own care

- Seeking another medical opinion

- Being informed of the fees associated with the visit

- Asking questions about available treatments, including their cost and effectiveness

- Discussing with your doctor any concerns or complaints

- Filing a grievance if you feel your concern or complaint was not handled adequately

- Terminating your care at any time, except if you are involuntarily hospitalized

How to Know If You Have a Good Doctor–Patient Fit

When you have good communication with your doctor, you are more likely to follow through with your treatment (Haskard Zolnierek and DiMatteo 2009). Here are some signs that you have a good relationship with your doctor:

- You feel comfortable asking questions.

- You feel you can be honest and open with your doctor.

- You feel comfortable and you trust the office staff.

- You feel your doctor listens to you and takes time to hear your concerns.

- You feel comfortable bringing up new or alternative treatments with your doctor.

- You feel okay calling your doctor's office with an urgent care question.

- Phone calls and messages are returned within a reasonable amount of time.

Preparing for the Appointment

Because people with ADD have difficulty remembering appointments, ask if the clinician's office can call to remind you the day before your appointment. In addition, print out a map of the route from your home to the clinician's office to ensure that you get there on time. Some clinician's offices will reschedule your appointment if you are fifteen minutes late, because having one patient show up late to an appointment can delay every patient's appointment for the rest of the day.

SUMMARY

In this chapter, you learned about the different types of mental health clinicians who are available to you as part of your ADD treatment team. There are prescribing clinicians, from whom you can receive medication for ADD, and nonprescribing clinicians, who do talk therapy or counseling. You also learned where to seek a recommendation or referral for a clinician, how to gather more information on a clinician, and how to go about scheduling an appointment. In the next chapter, you will learn about the evaluation and diagnosis process that mental health clinicians follow for determining if you have ADD.

CHAPTER 3

DIAGNOSIS

In chapter 2, you learned about the different types of clinicians who treat ADD and how to arrange a first appointment or evaluation. In this chapter, you will learn what that appointment might be like. You will learn what to bring with you to your appointment and discover issues related to filing a medical insurance claim for the visit. In addition, you will find out what happens during an evaluation for ADD, including what questions the doctor may ask and what testing you may be asked to complete. You will also learn the importance of knowing your family history of mental health issues. Finally, you will learn about the feelings you may experience after you have been diagnosed with ADD.

When you attend your first appointment with the clinician, it may be very similar to what is described in this chapter. Or it may be very different. Keep in mind that every clinician has their own style, or way of conducting an ADD evaluation. If you have any questions about the evaluation process, ask the clinician. Good clinicians encourage questions, and they answer patients' questions with respect.

BEFORE THE APPOINTMENT

You may have a flurry of questions and concerns before you even set foot in the clinician's office. This is completely normal. You may be wondering how long the appointment will take and what documents you should bring with you. You may also wonder if you should file a claim with your medical insurer.

How Long Will the Evaluation Take?

If you go to a clinician who specializes in mental health issues (a psychiatrist, nurse practitioner, counselor, or psychologist), your first appointment will typically last about an hour to an hour and a half. The length of your appointment depends on the type of clinician you see and how he schedules new-patient appointments.

Whom to Bring (or Not to Bring) with You

When you have ADD, your family and friends may be the best judge of the severity of your ADD symptoms (Quinlan 2000). It may be helpful to bring your spouse, partner, adult child, or parent with you to the appointment. Most clinicians are okay with you bringing a family member, although you should check ahead of time to see if this is okay. You may not want to bring your young children to the appointment, especially if they tend to be on the active side. If you are spending most of your time trying to corral your child, you won't be getting as much out of the appointment, and it may also frustrate the clinician. In addition, you will be discussing personal information with the clinician and may not want to talk about these things in front of your children.

What to Bring with You

In order to make your doctor's visit the most productive it can be, it is recommended that you bring the following items with you to the appointment. Be sure to review this checklist (and the details below) before you walk out your front door:

- Your current medication, in the original pill bottle(s)

- Past report cards or behavior reports

- Psychological testing reports

- Medical records

- Notes about your family's medical history

- Letters from family and friends

- A list of your concerns

- Workplace assessments and reviews

- A list outlining your job history

- Your medical insurance card

- Any forms the doctor's office sent you

CURRENT MEDICATION

Because you may be asked about your current medications—what you are taking, the dosage, and how often you take it—it is recommended that you bring your pill bottle(s) to your appointment. Any information your doctor needs about the medication is right there on the label.

DOCUMENTATION

Because you have had years of life experiences prior to this appointment, it is helpful to bring documentation from your school days and work experiences, medical records, and letters from your family members and friends. The more documentation you bring, the more information your clinician has to work with when determining a diagnosis. Also, don't worry if you feel like you have too much paperwork—just try to keep it as neat as possible by putting it in a folder. It's okay if the clinician doesn't look at all your paperwork—he will figure out what the most important papers are when you meet. Even if he just glances over some of your paperwork, he can still glean quite a bit of information.

Make sure you have the forms and other documentation prepared ahead of time. The night before your appointment, put the documents in a location you can see easily so you can grab them before you head out the door! You may even want to fax some of the documentation to the office ahead of time (let them know you will be doing this) to avoid arriving at the appointment without your documents.

Report cards and school reports. If you have any school records, bring them to your appointment. Your report cards may have had ADD-related comments on them such as "Doesn't work to potential," "Doesn't stay in seat," or even "Poor handwriting." In addition to the comments on your report cards, having *flipped grades* (receiving an A in science and a D in math one semester, then vice versa the next semester) may also be a sign of ADD. In addition to your report cards, bring in any documentation of school testing and any behavior reports. Also bring any paperwork related to receiving special services in the schools, such as an Individualized Education Program (IEP) or Section 504 Accommodations Form. Don't worry if you aren't able to bring in your report cards or other school records—if one or both of your parents have or had ADD, they may not have saved your report cards.

Workplace records. Bring any workplace assessments or reviews with you to your appointment. Your workplace reviews may have ADD-related statements from your employer such as "Difficulty getting to work on time," "Difficulty following through on assigned tasks," or "Does not meet deadlines." The assessments and reviews from your employer will also give your clinician a good idea about how many times you have changed jobs and for what reasons. It is also helpful to bring in a list of where you have worked, how long you worked at each job, and why you left. This information can be helpful to a clinician since people with ADD change jobs more frequently than those without ADD, and they are more likely to be fired for poor work performance (Barkley, Murphy, and Fischer 2008).

Notes about your family's medical history. Keep track of your family's medical history on a notepad so you can bring it to your clinician's appointment. See "Family History" for details about what to ask your family members.

Letters from family and friends. It can be helpful to bring your clinician letters from family members and friends describing their experiences with your ADD behaviors. You want the letters to be as descriptive as possible. Ask a person who knows you well to write a letter telling the story of a time when you had behavior issues or got yourself into trouble. You can also ask the person to mention tidbits about any other troublesome behaviors they have noticed in you over the years, such as having severe temper tantrums or getting into fights with your cousins. Every little bit of information helps.

It may be emotionally difficult for you to read the letters, because you will learn how others view your behavior. Keep in mind that the letter is being written to help you get the best care and most accurate diagnosis possible. As mentioned before, people around you may have a more accurate perception of the severity of your ADD symptoms than you do. That's just the nature of ADD—it is difficult to assess your own behavior.

To help your family and friends to provide useful responses, consider asking them the following questions:

- What have you noticed about my organizational skills, my follow-through on projects, my mood, and how I cope with day-to-day stress?

- What else have you noticed about my behavior?

- What areas of my life seem to be most affected?

- At what times do you notice that I'm doing better or don't seem to have as many difficulties?

- When did you first notice I had difficulties paying attention or sitting still?

- What are some of the impulsive things that I've done?

- How does my behavior affect you?

- What are some positive things you have noticed about me?

Should You File with Your Insurance Company?

First, you want to make sure that your medical insurance includes mental health benefits. You can find this information by reviewing the materials that came with your policy, visiting the insurer's website, or calling a customer service representative at the insurance company. Make sure that when you speak with a customer service representative, you get the information in writing—via e-mail, letter, or fax.

When you file an insurance claim for your evaluation or other appointments with your clinician, your clinician fills out a claim form. A diagnosis will be listed on the claim form because insurance companies require a diagnosis in order to pay a claim. If your clinician has diagnosed you with ADD, you may see something like "314.01 attention deficit hyperactivity disorder, combined type" either written or circled on the form you take to the office's checkout counter. The number "314.01" is a code in the *DSM-IV-TR* (2000) that clinicians use when diagnosing. You have the right to ask your clinician what diagnosis he is putting on the claim form if he has not told you already.

Be aware that any time you file a medical insurance claim, including claims for your visits to the clinician, that information is filed with a clearinghouse called the Medical Information Bureau (MIB). MIB states that the purpose of the bureau is to help prevent insurance fraud, but the claim information in your file may cause insurers to turn you down for medical, disability, or health insurance in the future. This is because the insurance company may deem you too risky to cover due to your past claim history—meaning that insurers may determine that you will wind up costing them more money than you pay for your insurance.

Because of issues that may arise, some patients choose to pay *out of pocket* when they see their clinician. This means they pay the full amount of their bill and do not file a claim with their medical insurance. While this may be a financial hardship for you, it does mean that no record of your visit will be in the MIB database. You do have a right to see the claims information that MIB has in your file. Contact information for MIB can be found in Resources at the end of this book.

WHEN YOU ARRIVE AT THE APPOINTMENT

When you arrive at the clinician's office (or even beforehand), you will be asked to fill out some forms. These forms will ask you for your name, address, and general identifying information. You may also be given a consent form that explains your rights as a patient and includes the office's policies, such as information about making payments and scheduling appointments. If the clinician's office files medical insurance claims, you will be asked to provide the insurer's contact information along with your medical insurance card so that the office can scan it or make a copy. The office may also have you fill out questionnaires about your current symptoms and medical history.

DURING THE APPOINTMENT

Now you are sitting in your clinician's office. What should you expect? The clinician will ask questions about your history of ADD symptoms and possibly alcohol, nicotine, and drug use as well as your family history of mental health. You may also be asked to complete some assessments to further help the clinician make a determination or diagnosis. Finally, questions may arise in your own mind during your appointment.

Questions About Alcohol, Nicotine, or Drug Use

Your clinician may ask about your current and past use of alcohol, nicotine, and drugs. Answer these questions truthfully, because your clinician may want to prescribe different medications if you have a history of abuse or addiction. Remember, clinicians have heard it all before. Very little that you say can shock them. If you do feel upset about a clinician's response, address that with her. Remember, if things don't "click" with that particular clinician, you can always go to another.

As mentioned, it is recommended that you bring your pill bottles with you as your doctor may also ask you what medications you are taking as well as how much and how often. The pill bottle label provides most of the information your doctor needs; you may also be asked what benefits and side effects you may have from your medications.

If you feel uncomfortable answering any of the clinician's questions, tell her your concerns. Remember, however, the questions the clinician asks are a way for her to better understand you and your life experiences in order to make a more accurate diagnosis. Because there are no definitive tests for ADD like there are for other medical disorders, the diagnosis is subjective. This means that your clinician's diagnosis is at least partially dependent on the information you provide.

Family History

Because ADD and other mental health disorders are genetic, your clinician may ask you for your family's history of mental health issues. For clinicians, family members fall into two categories: *first-degree* and *second-degree* relatives. First-degree relatives are those most closely genetically related to you—your parents, your siblings, and your children. Second-degree relatives include your grandparents, aunts, uncles, and cousins.

Before your appointment, ask your family about the following mental health issues in addition to ADD:

- Anxiety

- Depression

- Bipolar disorder or mania

- Schizophrenia

- Alcohol use/abuse

- Drug use/abuse

- Any psychiatric hospitalizations

- Attempted or committed suicide

As mentioned above, keep track of this information on a notepad so you can bring it to your clinician's appointment. You want to find out from family members about relatives who were diagnosed with ADD by a clinician and also about those who were considered "off" or "different" by their loved ones. Keep in mind that if ADD runs rampant in your family, no one may notice the ADD symptoms in a relative because it seems so normal!

If you are adopted, you may not have access to information about your biological family. If you know the circumstances of your adoption or any characteristics of your biological family, every bit of information helps. Particularly important is any information you have pertaining to a possible history of ADD or other mental health issues.

Testing and Assessments

While you are at your evaluation appointment, your clinician may ask you to complete testing (assessments), to further aid in determining a diagnosis. These assessments are another way for your clinician to get information on your symptoms and experiences. They can also act as a tool to help your clinician eliminate (that is, rule out) other diagnoses such as bipolar disorder. While there is not one definitive test that can diagnose ADD, these tests can be a valuable part of the overall evaluation process, providing your clinician with more pieces to the puzzle. There are two main types of assessments for ADD: rating scales and tests of working memory.

RATING SCALES

Rating scales measure your current ADD symptoms and childhood symptoms—the total number of symptoms and the frequency and severity of each. Some of the rating scales you fill out yourself, such as the Adult ADHD Self-Report Scale (ASRS; Kessler et al. 2005) and the Current Symptoms Scale and Childhood Symptoms Scale (Barkley and Murphy 1998). The clinician will fill out some of the scales as she talks with you; these include the ADHD Rating Scale-IV (ADD-RS-IV; DuPaul et al. 1998), the Brown Attention-Deficit Disorder Scales (Brown 1996), and the Wender Utah Rating Scale (Ward, Wender, and Reimherr 1993). Be as honest and open as possible. As mentioned previously in this chapter, the more information you give your clinician, the better able she is to help you.

As you read earlier in this chapter, family members often have a more accurate view then you do of your behaviors and their impact on your quality of life. Therefore, your clinician may also give you rating scales for your family members to fill out regarding your childhood and current ADD symptoms. You return the scales at your next appointment.

TESTS OF WORKING MEMORY

As you learned in chapter 1, the frontal lobes of the brain perform the executive functions. These functions are impaired when you have ADD. One of the executive functions is called *working memory*. Working memory is the ability to hold information, process it, and put the information back out again. The more severe your ADD symptoms are, the more difficulty you may have on tasks where you have to use your working memory.

During your evaluation appointment, your clinician may want you to take a test of your working memory. Tests of working memory can be of different types. One type is the "continuous performance test" (CPT), where you are asked to pay attention for a long period of time while you perform a task that tests your working memory processes.

The Integrated Visual and Auditory CPT (IVA+Plus) is a CPT that you take on a computer (Sandford and Turner 2004). The test measures your verbal and auditory attention capabilities. During the test, you are asked to press the space bar every time you see a number "1" or hear the word "one." The test measures how many times you hit the space bar accurately, how many times you hit it inaccurately, how long it took you to hit the space bar, and other variables.

Another task of working memory is called the Tower of London (or Tower of Hanoi) (Culbertson and Zillmer 1999). In this task, you have a board with three pegs of different sizes, in addition to beads of different colors. Your job is to match the bead patterns that the tester (or computer program) demonstrates for you. There are rules you must follow for this task, and you are timed by the tester or computer for each of the patterns.

While taking the IVA+Plus or the computerized Tower of London test, you are usually sitting in a room by yourself with limited distractions. This is because outside distractions might change the results of the test and make it a less accurate measure of your ADD symptoms.

You may also be asked to take other tests of working memory function: a Stroop test and a Trail-Making Test (Reynolds 2002; Trenerry et al. 1989). The Stroop test consists of names of colors written in an ink that is different from the color name. You are asked to say the color of the word, not the word itself. For example, the word "yellow" may be written in blue. Therefore, the correct answer would be "blue." People with ADD tend to have difficulty with this task because the frontal lobe of your brain has difficulties inhibiting (or stopping) itself from saying the word, not the color of the word.

The Trail-Making Test consists of two parts. In Part A, twenty-five circles are on a sheet of paper. Every circle has a number in it, from one to twenty-five. Your task is to connect the numbers in order. In Part B, there are twenty-five circles with numbers in them, and there are also circles with letters in them. Your task is to connect the circles in this way: 1-A-2-B and so on. You are not allowed to lift the pen or pencil from the paper, and you are timed by the tester.

Don't worry if you get bored or your brain gets tired during these tests. That is one of the purposes of the working memory tests—to see how your brain reacts to long and repetitive tasks.

It is very normal for an ADD brain to feel tired during and/ or after one of these tests. However, give it your best shot and try to get through the whole thing. The more information your doctor receives from this testing, the more she can help you.

If you are prescribed medication for ADD, your clinician may ask you to take the same test(s) again at a later appointment while the medication is in your system. The results of the later test, when compared to your *baseline* (original) test, will give the clinician an indication of how well your medication is working. Based in part on this information, your clinician may consider increasing or decreasing the dose of your medication or change your medication altogether. Let your doctor know if you have forgotten to take your medication that day or if you took your medication immediately before your appointment. Otherwise the results of your testing may not be entirely accurate.

MOTION TRACKING TESTS

Another type of ADD assessment is a computerized test that measures your amount of movement while you are sitting in a chair doing a working memory task. One of these motion tracking tests is called the Quotient™ ADHD System (Teicher 2008). This assessment measures both your physical movements (such as squirming in your chair and being restless) and your working memory ability. Two infrared scanners track your movements for twenty minutes while you take the computerized test. These types of assessments are less common due to their cost and the extra space in the clinician's office that they require.

BRAIN SCANS

You may have read about the use of brain scans, like single photon emission computed tomography (SPECT) to determine an ADD diagnosis. However, as of the printing of this book, there is not enough research to recommend this as a definitive test of ADD. In addition, these scans can be expensive and you might have to travel quite a distance to obtain one. For the majority of people, the lack of scientific evidence outweighs the cost.

Commonly Asked Questions About Being Diagnosed with ADD

During your appointment, you may find yourself asking the following questions.

HOW DOES THE CLINICIAN REALLY KNOW I HAVE ADD?

As was mentioned earlier in this chapter, there is no definitive test for ADD or any other mental health disorder. This is why it is important to give the clinician as much information and documentation as possible. Yes, sometimes misdiagnoses are made, but going to a clinician is a positive first step in getting your questions answered accurately and thoroughly.

HOW MUCH TIME IS NEEDED TO MAKE AN ADD DIAGNOSIS?

It depends. If you have been seeing this clinician for a while, and she knows your family (and your family history), then you may not need to see her for as long as you would if you were a new patient. However, if you are at the clinician's office and you just feel like he hasn't taken enough time with you, it is important that you mention that to him. In essence, it's not so much the amount of time spent doing the evaluation as whether you feel like you received a complete evaluation.

HOW OFTEN DO I NEED TO COME BACK TO THE CLINICIAN?

If you have been prescribed medication, your clinician will most likely want you to return for a "medication management" appointment. Usually these are scheduled for once a month at first; when you are on an effective dose of medication, the visits are reduced to once every three months. However, this can differ depending on how well the medication is working or if you have any side effects.

WHAT IF I DON'T AGREE WITH THE CLINICIAN?

As described at the end of chapter 2, there are ways to know if you have a good doctor–patient fit. But what if you don't agree with something the clinician said or did? The best way to handle it is to mention your concern to her while you are still at your appointment. If after taking this first step—talking to the clinician—your concerns are not answered to your satisfaction, you have other options:

- You can always get a second opinion from another clinician.

- If you feel the clinician has violated ethics or laws, you can contact the clinician's professional organization or the state licensing board.

Again, the important thing is that you talk to the clinician first before taking these other measures.

AFTER YOUR DIAGNOSIS

Once your clinician confirms that you meet the diagnostic criteria for ADD, you may experience a flood of different feelings, like shock, relief, hope, or even disappointment or grief. It is important to remember that everyone experiences the news of their diagnosis in a different way. How you experience these feelings depends on the severity of your ADD, how much your life has been affected by having it, and the amount of support that you receive from your family and friends. You may experience all, some, or none of the following stages, and you may experience them in a different order than is given here. You will learn more about getting support from others in chapter 7.

The Light Bulb or "Aha!" Stage

When you realize that you have ADD, finally (and suddenly) everything makes sense. You may start medication or counseling. You may also start noticing your ADD behaviors more—they may even seem to be getting worse. What used to be a mild difficulty with managing clutter now becomes glaringly obvious to you. You wonder if maybe being diagnosed with ADD or starting medication has made your ADD worse. What's really going on is only that paying more attention to your symptoms can make them *seem* worse.

The "What Do I Do Now?" Stage

During this stage, you may start debating whether you want to get treatment for your ADD. You may start questioning the usefulness or safety of medication. You may also wonder if you should share with your family and friends that you have been diagnosed with ADD. You may wonder if it would be wise to share your diagnosis with your employer, and if you do, how it may affect your job. You may feel overwhelmed by all the decisions you think need to be made before you can move forward.

The "Life Could Have Been Easier" Stage

During this stage, you may beat yourself up over things that you did in the past. You may also feel a sense of loss over "how much easier things would have been" if you had received treatment earlier. You might even feel anger toward your parents, teachers, and other caregivers for not getting you help earlier for your ADD symptoms. Keep in mind that they did the best they could with the knowledge, resources, and information they had at the time. The important thing is that today is a new day, and now you have found the missing puzzle piece to your life. It is important to forgive yourself and your parents, caregivers, and teachers.

The "Stocking Up on Info" Stage

You are now hungry for more information on ADD. You want to find out where all these other ADD people are and where to get tips on how to deal with ADD. You may join a support organization, such as CHADD or ADDA, mentioned in chapter 2. You may participate in an Internet forum like Attention Deficit Hyperactivity Disorder Forums. You may also start reading books and Internet articles on ADD.

The "Making Changes" Stage

You may more actively rally your friends and family around you for support. (You will learn more about the support available to you in chapter 7.) You may also discontinue relationships with people who you feel "just don't get" your diagnosis of ADD. You may be less tolerant of those who feel that ADD is not a valid diagnosis. You may feel anger or frustration toward friends or family members who tell you that you shouldn't be taking medication. You may also find that your relationships have changed because your ADD symptoms are getting better.

The "New Me" or Acceptance Stage

You may openly tell people that you have ADD. You've made peace with your past experiences. You see ADD as a part of you, but you are aware that it doesn't define your entire identity. You are not just a person with ADD—you are also a mother, father, daughter, spouse, partner, coworker, employee—take your pick! If you take medication, you are taking it regularly and as prescribed. You may now be working to educate others about ADD and may become an advocate for yourself in school, at home, or in the workplace.

I had a sense of relief that I finally had a diagnosis of what was causing many of the issues I experienced in life. But [I] also had a sense of guilt and regret about the lost opportunities. Now I am pleased with my treatment and relieved that I can focus on researching and understanding how ADD impacts my life.

—Michael

SUMMARY

In this chapter, you learned about what happens before, during, and after your initial appointment, or evaluation, for ADD. You learned what to bring with you to your appointment and whether you should file a claim with your medical insurer. You also discovered the questions you might be asked during an evaluation, the importance of knowing your family history of ADD, and the types of assessments you might be asked to complete. Finally, you learned about the different feelings or stages you might experience after you have been diagnosed with ADD. In the next chapter, you will learn about treatments available for ADD, including medication, counseling, and coaching.

CHAPTER 4

—※———————————————————※—

TREATMENTS
FOR ADD

After being diagnosed with ADD, one of the positives you'll discover is that there is help available. In this chapter, you will learn about some of the treatment options available for ADD, including medication, counseling, neurofeedback, and coaching. For each treatment, you will learn the possible benefits and risks. You will also find information on the studies behind each treatment.

Having ADD is like climbing up a mountain with a back-pack full of rocks. You can make it to the top of the mountain, but it's going to take a lot of extra energy and time. When you get effective treatment for ADD, you're getting some of the rocks out of your backpack. While treatment doesn't get rid of all of the rocks, it makes the climb much more manageable.

Treatment allows you to work at a more even pace with your non-ADD coworkers and helps you feel more like you are an active participant in your life. Knowing you need additional help for ADD is a sign of strength, not a weakness.

HOW TO CHOOSE THE BEST TREATMENT

When looking at treatments, ask yourself if the benefits of the treatment outweigh the risks. Is the potential for improvement from this treatment worth its cost? How much time must be invested for this course of treatment? What are the possible side effects?

Do your research. What do you know about the treatment? What is the training of the clinicians providing the treatment? If someone tells you he or she has a "cure" for ADD, or gives you a guarantee, run the other way. There is no known cure for ADD at this time, and no treatment—no matter how many studies back it up—is 100 percent guaranteed. In addition, a treatment that is effective for one person may not work for another. The amount and intensity of ADD symptoms varies from person to person. If a particular treatment doesn't work, there are others available.

MEDICATION

Because ADD is a biological disorder and involves a deficiency of brain chemicals, medication remains the most effective treatment for ADD. As you learned in chapter 1, the ADD brain has low levels of a neurotransmitter called dopamine. Medication replaces or renews the neurotransmitters the ADD brain lacks. Medication is a tool for better living—it helps you access and use coping techniques that can improve your quality of life. You may find that medication helps you benefit even more from counseling or a support group because now you can fully pay attention. While medications do not "cure" ADD or completely reduce your symptoms, they can help you function better at work, at home, and in social situations.

Do You Need Medication?

You may be making decisions about whether you really need to consider additional help like medication as a treatment for ADD. Here are some questions to ask yourself:

- Do you find that you have to work at least twice as hard as your coworkers but still can't finish your assignments?

- Do you forget to review your work and, as a result, make careless mistakes?

- Do you feel that you are a chronic underachiever and you just haven't worked to your potential?

- Have you injured yourself due to inattention or to impulsive or daredevil behavior?

- Have you gotten into legal or financial trouble due to your impulsivity?

- Do you have difficulty maintaining healthy relationships and friendships because of your short fuse, distractibility, lack of social skills, or impulsiveness?

- Have you tried other treatments for ADD, like counseling and coaching, but still have room for improvement?

- Do you have family members who have ADD, and have they received positive results from medication?

You might want to show this list of questions to your friends and family and ask them for their opinions. Because people with ADD can have difficulty judging the severity of their behavior, the people closest to you may have a more accurate view of how you are functioning. The more questions you answered yes to, the more you may benefit from ADD medication treatment.

> *I have doubts about whether I would have made it*
> *[to where I am now], two-thirds of the way through*
> *law school, without medication. Sitting down to*
> *study every day would have been impossible before.*
> *Medication has even helped with smaller issues—*
> *like locking myself out of my house and car on such*
> *a regular basis that I had a locksmith on speed dial.*
>
> —Lauren

Types of Medication for ADD

There are two different types or classes of medication approved by the U.S. Food and Drug Administration (FDA) for the treatment of ADD: *stimulants* and *nonstimulants*. When these medications are labeled "FDA approved," it means that the FDA is satisfied with the data from scientific studies showing that a medication is a safe and effective treatment for ADD. FDA approval also means that the pharmaceutical company is allowed to market and advertise that medication for the treatment of ADD. Keep in mind that even if a medication is not FDA-approved for ADD, it can still legally be prescribed by your doctor and may be an effective treatment.

STIMULANTS

Stimulants increase attention, decrease hyperactivity, and decrease impulsivity by stimulating the frontal lobes of the brain and raising dopamine levels. Methylphenidate and dextro-amphetamines are stimulants that are FDA-approved for treating ADD. The most noticeable side effects of stimulants are decreased appetite, headaches, and difficulty sleeping. In rare cases, people may develop tics (involuntary movements) after taking stimulants.

Stimulants are classified as *Schedule II medications* by the FDA. This means that stimulant medications are *controlled substances*, medications that have a mild addictive potential. Some people abuse stimulants for their side effects, such as increased alertness and weight loss. Because of the potential for abuse, stimulant medications cannot be called into a pharmacy by your doctor—you have to pick up the prescription at the doctor's office or have it mailed directly to you.

If you take your stimulant medication as prescribed, there is a low potential for addiction. In fact, as will be noted later in this chapter, appropriate use of stimulant medication may actually reduce your chances of developing a substance abuse problem.

There are two types of stimulants: extended-release and immediate-release.

Extended-release stimulants are effective for eight to twelve hours, so you just have to take your medication once a day. Extended-release stimulants include Concerta (methylphenidate HCl extended-release), Vyvanse (lisdexamfetamine), Daytrana (methylphenidate transdermal), Focalin XR (dexmethylpheni-date extended-release), Adderall XR (mixed salts of a single-entity amphetamine product extended-release), and Dexedrine Spansules sustained-release capsules (dextroamphetamine).

Immediate-release stimulants, such as Ritalin (methylpheni-date), Focalin (dexmethylphenidate), and Dexedrine (dextroam-phetamine), last three to four hours. If you need to take your medication while you are at work, at school, or traveling, carry a small amount of your medication in the original pill bottle.

Drug testing and stimulant medications. If you are taking stimulant medication and have to take a drug test, your urine will test positive for amphetamines, even if you have stopped taking your stimulant medication prior to the test. Carry a small amount of your medication in the original pill bottle and have a signed note from your doctor. The note should say you are prescribed stimulant medication for ADD, give the name of the medication, and explain that a drug test could be positive for amphetamines due to this medication.

Addiction and stimulant medications. Stimulant medications are regulated by the FDA and are prescribed at low doses. They are not addictive if they are taken as prescribed. In fact, some studies have shown that stimulant medication does not increase or decrease the rate of developing substance abuse, while other studies have shown that people with ADD who take stimulant medication actually have a much lower rate of substance abuse than people with ADD who do not take medication (Biederman, Monuteaux, et al. 2008; Biederman 2003; Wilens et al. 2003). This may be because people who take medication for their ADD now have a safe way of increasing the level of dopamine in the brain rather than trying to feel better by using illegal drugs.

NONSTIMULANTS

There are currently two nonstimulants that are FDA-approved for the treatment of ADD—Strattera (atomoxetine) and Intuniv (guanfacine extended-release). Sometimes these nonstimulant medications are prescribed along with stimulant medication to treat ADD.

Strattera (atomoxetine). In 2002, Strattera was the first non-stimulant approved by the FDA for the treatment of ADD. Strattera is different from a stimulant in that it is chemically more like an antidepressant. It is in a class of medications called *selective norepinephrine reuptake inhibitors* (SNRIs). This means that the medication allows more *norepinephrine* (a neurotransmitter) to linger in the spaces between neurons.

Strattera has been found to significantly decrease the severity of hyperactive and inattentive symptoms in adults when compared to a *placebo* (sugar pill) (Newcorn et al. 2008). Strattera can be helpful for people who have not had success with stimulant medication or for those who have depression and anxiety in addition to ADD (Hammerness et al. 2009; Vaughan, Fegert, and Kratochvil 2009). Strattera is not addictive, so, unlike stimulant medications, it is not a Schedule II drug. The most common side effects of Strattera are stomach upset, dry mouth, and decreased appetite.

Intuniv (guanfacine extended-release). In 2009, Intuniv was FDA approved for the treatment of ADD. Intuniv interacts with receptors in the prefrontal cortex of the brain. Intuniv has been found to significantly reduce hyperactivity, impulsivity, and inattentiveness as compared to a placebo (sugar pill) (Biederman, Melmed, et al. 2008). Side effects include low blood pressure, low heart rate, fainting, and drowsiness. In addition, you may have to take Intuniv for up to two weeks before you see benefits.

OTHER MEDICATIONS

While Wellbutrin XL (bupropion HCl extended-release) and Provigil (modafinil) are not currently FDA-approved for the treatment of ADD, they have shown some effectiveness in treating the symptoms.

Wellbutrin XL (bupropion HCl extended-release). Wellbutrin XL is a *norepinephrine and dopamine reuptake inhibitor* (NDRI). It is an antidepressant. Like Strattera, this medication allows more norepinephrine to linger between the neurons. In addition, it also allows dopamine to share that space. Wellbutrin XL is FDA-indicated for depression but not for ADD. However, it has shown promise in helping reduce ADD symptoms in adults (Wigal 2009; Solhkhah et al. 2005). Side effects include dry mouth, headaches, and nausea. In rare cases, seizures may occur, particularly in people who have a history of eating disorders. You will learn more about eating disorders in chapter 5.

Provigil (modafinil). Provigil is a long-acting stimulant that is currently FDA-approved to treat narcolepsy, a disorder that makes it difficult for people to stay awake. Some doctors prescribe this medication for ADD. Provigil may activate nerve cells in a part of the brain called the hypothalamus, although the exact way Provigil works is not known. Side effects of Provigil include headache, nausea, dizziness, and trouble sleeping. Provigil has shown some evidence that it improves ADD symptoms, and it can be helpful to adults with ADD who have not had success with other medications (Lindsay, Gudelsky, and Heaton 2006). A new, longer-lasting formulation of Provigil, called Nuvigil (armodafinil), was approved by the FDA in 2007.

HERBAL SUPPLEMENTS

Herbal supplements are pills or powders made from naturally occurring ingredients. Sometimes people look to herbal supplements as an alternative to prescribed medication. However, be aware that there is little scientific evidence that herbal supplements are effective in treating ADD (Sawni 2008). Also be aware that herbal supplements are not required to have FDA approval before being put on the market. In addition, some studies have found that the concentration of an herbal supplement can vary greatly from product to product (Curtis and Gaylord 2005; Rotblatt 1999). For these reasons, make sure the supplement's manufacturer adheres to strict quality-control measures—for example, by choosing to follow the FDA's Good Manufacturing Practice (GMP) regulations (Frankos, Street, and O'Neill 2010); you may see "GMP" on an herbal supplement label, if so.

Make sure you tell your doctor if you are considering taking herbal supplements or if you are already taking them. Some herbal supplements, including kava kava, valerian root, and St. John's wort, interact with your body's central nervous system, can interact with your medication, and can affect the way your body absorbs medication (Mitra et al. 2010; Izzo and Ernst 2009; Foti, Wahlstrom, and Wienkers 2007).

OMEGA-3 AND OMEGA-6 FATTY ACIDS

There is evidence that omega-3 fatty acids can help improve the symptoms of ADD. Studies have found that people with ADD had a significantly lower level of omega-3 fatty acids in their blood than people without ADD (Schuchardt et al. 2010; Antalis et al. 2006). Fish oil and polyunsaturated fatty acids, which contain omega-3 and omega-6, have been found to increase this level (Sinn and Bryan 2007; Young, Conquer, and Thomas 2005). ADD symptoms improved somewhat in children who were taking both omega-3 and omega-6 supplements (Transler et al. 2010).

Commonly Asked Questions About Medication for ADD

It is completely normal for you to have questions about ADD medication. You are always encouraged to talk to your doctor about any questions or concerns. Here are five of the most commonly asked questions about medication.

DO I HAVE TO TAKE MEDICATION FOR THE REST OF MY LIFE?

It is virtually impossible to know what will happen to you in the future—many people function much better on medication and continue to take it so that they can have the best quality of life possible. Others decide that they want to stop their medication to see if they still "need" it anymore. If you do decide to discontinue your medication, make sure you talk with your doctor first. You don't want to stop ADD medications abruptly, particularly some nonstimulant medications. Your doctor will know how to safely decrease your dosage so you are less likely to experience side effects from discontinuation.

After stopping, some people decide they want to get back on their medication, while some decide that medication is no longer something they feel they need. It can be helpful to give yourself a "window" of two weeks after you stop your medication. After this time, check in with yourself and your family to see how you are doing. You may notice even before those two weeks are up that your medication really was helping you. It is okay to realize that you do need medication in order to function to your full potential.

WHY IS THE DOCTOR CHANGING MY MEDICATION (AGAIN)?

There is no blood test for ADD like tests for other medical disorders, such as diabetes. So finding an ideal medication for you can involve trial and error, and that's why your doctor may need to change your dosage amount, or even your medication, so you can receive the most benefits and the least amount of side effects. There are several different medications available, and if one is causing problems for you, another might work better. It is very important to tell your doctor how your medication is affecting you—he will then be able to help you.

Remember, it may take a few weeks or more before you notice the benefits of some medications, particularly nonstimulant medication. Also, your doctor may start you out on a low dose and gradually increase it, so you may not notice a lot of changes right away. Remember to be patient and keep open lines of communication with your doctor.

HOW CAN I REMEMBER TO TAKE MY MEDICATION?

The more severe your ADD symptoms, the less likely it is that you will take your medication regularly (Safren et al. 2007). You may forget to take your medication due to forgetfulness and distraction, or you may avoid taking it because of unwanted side effects. You are more likely to remember your medication if you are receiving more benefits than side effects.

In order to remember to take your medication, buy a weekly pill container, which is divided into sections that are labeled by the day of the week. The container helps you remember to take your medicine and also prevents you from taking it twice. You may be able to get a pill container for free from your pharmacy or doctor's office. It is much easier to remember to fill your pill container when you do it on the same day every week. In addition, filling up more than one day of the week at one time is even more efficient.

Another way to remember your medication is to take it at the same time every day. Set an alarm, such as on your cell phone, to remind you. By taking your medication at the same time every day, not only are you getting into a good habit, but you are also making sure that your medication is evenly dosed in your body within every twenty-four-hour cycle.

IF I DIDN'T LIKE TAKING MEDICATIONS WHEN I WAS A CHILD, WHY TRY AGAIN?

It is important to figure out why you didn't have a good experience with medications when you were a child. Was it because someone was "making" you take a medication? Did you experience side effects? Did you have to leave your classroom every day so you could take your medication at the nurse's office?

No one can force you to take medication for ADD now that you are an adult. The choice is completely up to you. In addition, medications have improved since you were a child. Newer medications have more benefits and fewer side effects. As you learned earlier in this chapter, medications are now available in an extended-release formulation. This means you only have to take one pill a day. People who take extended-release formulations may experience fewer side effects as compared to the immediate-release formulations, due to the more even amount of medication being released in the body from hour to hour throughout the day (McGough et al. 2003).

If you took stimulant medications for ADD when you were a child, there is good news. A study by Biederman and colleagues (2009) found that adults with ADD who took stimulant medications as children functioned better both socially and psychologically as compared to those with ADD who did not take stimulant medication as children. Children who took stimulant medication for ADD were also significantly less likely to develop depression and anxiety disorders later in life (Biederman et al. 2009).

When you meet with your doctor, make sure you are honest with him about your experiences with medications in the past. Tell your doctor which medications you took and how they made you feel—this information can affect what your doctor prescribes for you. If you are not sure what medications you took, ask your parents or see if any of your previous medical records are available.

ISN'T TAKING MEDICATION JUST A CRUTCH?

ADD is a genetic and biological disorder, just as diabetes is. You wouldn't tell someone that taking insulin is a crutch! You may feel like you should be able to "conquer" ADD on your own and not need any treatment. But remember, when you have ADD, you have a low level of the neurotransmitter dopamine in your brain. Medication is a relatively safe and effective way of allowing your brain to get the missing neurotransmitters it needs. Medication can help you reach your potential and be the person you know you could be.

OTHER ADD TREATMENTS

Counseling, neurofeedback, and coaching may provide additional relief from your symptoms, even if you are not taking medication. While there is more scientific evidence for the effectiveness of prescription medication than for these alternative treatments, more research is being conducted.

Counseling

You may have tried improving your relationships or quality of life on your own and you may feel you still aren't making much progress. A professional (and neutral) third party may be able to help you figure out solutions to your ADD-related challenges. Sometimes it can be very helpful just to have someone listen to you without judging you. You may want to talk about how ADD has affected your life, including discussing any lingering feelings of anger or sadness.

Counseling can do more than just help you; it can also help your marital or long-term relationship and your relationship with your family. There are mental health clinicians who are licensed specifically in marriage and family counseling. There are other mental health clinicians who have received additional training in marriage and family therapy.

WHAT TECHNIQUES DO COUNSELORS USE?

Some mental health clinicians have training in *cognitive behavioral therapy* (CBT), a therapeutic approach. CBT can be useful in treating adult ADD (Salakari et al. 2010; Solanto et al. 2010; Safren et al. 2005). One benefit of CBT is that you can learn how your beliefs about a situation have an impact on how you respond to it. For example, if you were told in school that you weren't as smart as the other children, you may automatically tell yourself "I can't do this" when faced with a challenging task. In CBT, you learn new *self-talk* that can make a difference in how you respond to and benefit from a situation. "I can't do this" becomes "I can complete this task successfully" or "I'll try my best."

QUESTIONS AND CONCERNS ABOUT COUNSELING

Keep in mind that counseling is not a cure-all for your issues. Counseling is like a lot of other things in life—you get out of it what you put into it. If you feel that you do not "click" with a counselor, there are others to choose from. It can be normal to interview a few counselors before you sense a good fit. As you learned in chapter 2, when you are seeking a counselor, ask her how much experience she has in working with adult ADD clients. Also ask her for her opinion of the ADD diagnosis and how she feels about the use of medication as a treatment for

ADD. Make sure that her viewpoint on both these topics aligns with yours.

If you have any questions about a counselor's therapeutic techniques or training, ask her. Also tell her if you are concerned about anything she has recommended or said during the session. Good counselors appreciate questions and feedback. For more information on finding a counselor, see chapter 2 and Resources at the end of this book.

Neurofeedback

The ADD brain and non-ADD brain have different theta and beta brain wave patterns. The purpose of neurofeedback is to teach a person how to change her brain waves by controlling a computer game with her mind. Sensors are placed on your scalp and by each ear. The sensors are connected to a device that creates an *electroencephalogram* (EEG), a reading of your brain waves. The therapist (or other person administering the neurofeedback) can tell how the brain is reacting by viewing the EEG. When someone with ADD has a decrease in theta waves and an increase in beta waves, that person can become more focused yet also more relaxed. It seems almost counterintuitive, but the more you teach your brain to relax, the more it can pay attention.

Neurofeedback treatments can be expensive, and full treatment requires several visits. In addition, there are limited studies that show its long-term effectiveness in treating ADD. However, in some studies, neurofeedback has been shown to be more effective than not receiving any treatment (Gevensleben et al. 2009). Just like the SPECT scans that were mentioned in chapter 3, if you can afford this treatment and it works for you, that is wonderful. For many people, however, the chances of improvement do not outweigh the potential cost of the sessions.

Coaching

Coaching is like "counseling lite." In coaching sessions, you are learning how to establish goals, set priorities, and get organized rather than talking about your past and your feelings. Coaches can meet with you in person, and some conduct coaching sessions online. Some coaches may even come to your house or workplace so they can get a better sense of your lifestyle and the areas in which you need help. Coaches can teach you coping skills and help you get your space organized. When you are working on a task, a coach can help you set manageable deadlines, and you can check in with your coach to report your progress. This makes you more accountable for how much work you are getting done.

There are some certification programs for ADD coaches, although a certificate is not required. In addition, there are currently no state licenses for ADD coaches. When seeking a coach, ask for referrals and ask the coach about his specific experiences working with ADD clients. You can find information on coaching in Resources at the end of this book.

SUMMARY

In this chapter, you learned about some of the treatment options available for ADD—medication, counseling, neurofeedback, and coaching. Which treatment you choose is completely up to you—each treatment has benefits and side effects. The best method for determining your chosen course of treatment is to educate yourself about the options. In the next chapter, you will learn about some of the issues that are more common when you have ADD—substance abuse, depression, anxiety, and eating disorders.

CHAPTER 5

ADDITIONAL CONCERNS WHEN YOU HAVE ADD

A diagnosis of ADD may bring other concerns into focus. When you have ADD, you are more prone to having a substance abuse problem. In addition to substance abuse, people with ADD also have a higher rate of depression, anxiety, and eating disorders, which can lead to more difficulties with day-to-day functioning and may require additional medication treatment (Spencer 2009). When you have another disorder in addition to ADD, it is called a *comorbid disorder*. This just means that you are experiencing ADD and something else at the same time. In this chapter, you will learn about each of these issues, including how to get help for them so you can live a happier and more productive life.

SELF-MEDICATION AND ITS EFFECTS

People with ADD are more likely than those without ADD to abuse alcohol and other drugs, including caffeine, nicotine, alcohol, marijuana, and cocaine—in fact, one in five ADD adults has experienced substance abuse (Wilens and Upadhyaya 2007). There is also a much higher rate of ADD in addicts than in the general population (Wilens et al. 2006). People with ADD also start using drugs at an earlier age and have more intense use than people without ADD (Wilens et al. 2005). Not only do people with ADD have an increased risk of addiction, it is also more difficult for people with ADD to quit (and stay substance-free).

As you read in chapter 1, when you have ADD, you are lacking a brain chemical, the neurotransmitter dopamine. If your brain chemicals are low, you will find a way to replace those chemicals, whether you do so consciously or unconsciously. This can result in using, abusing, and eventually becoming dependent on drugs like caffeine, nicotine, alcohol, marijuana, cocaine, and prescription drugs. In fact, some of these drugs do help you to focus and feel like your brain is "normal" for a short period of time. However, those effects do not last and can cause some nasty withdrawal symptoms when you try to stop. As you learned in chapter 4, prescribed medication is a safer, regulated, and less addictive way to help your brain get the chemicals it needs.

There has been an increase in diagnosed and undiagnosed ADD adults, especially younger adults seeking addiction treatment. Many addicted clients have treated their ADD unknowingly with mind-altering substances.

—Kelly Aissen, Ph.D., NCC, LMHC

Caffeine

People with ADD are twice as likely to use caffeine as people without ADD (Walker, Abraham, and Tercyak 2010). The truth is that caffeine *does* help you focus—but only for about a half hour. The side effects of caffeine withdrawal last much longer than the beneficial effects. Caffeine withdrawal symptoms include stomachaches, irritable bowel problems, headaches, vomiting, nervousness, and insomnia. If you plan on weaning yourself off of caffeine, it is recommended that you drink a little less each day instead of stopping abruptly. This will help reduce withdrawal symptoms. Consult with your doctor before cutting back on your caffeine use, especially if you have been using large amounts of caffeine for an extended period of time.

Nicotine

People with ADD start smoking at a younger age, smoke more cigarettes per day, and have a harder time quitting the habit (Ribeiro et al. 2008). The more severe your ADD symptoms, the more likely it is that you will be a regular smoker (Kollins, McClernon, and Fuemmeler 2005). Smokers who have ADD also have a greater risk of using other drugs (Biederman et al. 2006). If you would like to quit smoking, there are medications available, including Wellbutrin/Zyban (bupropion HCl), Chantix (varenicline), and nicotine patches and gum. Stimulant medication and nicotine patches can help you cease smoking, both when used by themselves and when used together (Gehricke et al. 2006). Methods such as hypnosis and counseling may also help you quit smoking, especially if they are combined with nicotine replacement therapy (Carmody et al. 2008). One of the bonuses of quitting is that lung damage caused by smoking may be reversed, depending on how long, and how much, you have been smoking. Consult your doctor if you are considering quitting.

Alcohol

If you have ADD, you are more likely to abuse alcohol than people who do not have ADD, at a rate of 18.5 to 5.3 percent (Barkley, Murphy, and Fischer 2008). In addition, approximately 35 to 71 percent of alcoholics have ADD (Wilens 2004). Chronic alcohol abuse can lead to cirrhosis (liver damage), increased difficulties paying attention, and, in extreme cases, death.

You particularly want to be careful about your alcohol consumption when you are taking certain medications for ADD. For example, if you are taking stimulant medications, you may not experience the usual effect of your alcohol intake until your medication wears off. Then you may suddenly feel the impact of how much you have had to drink. But even if you don't feel a "buzz" from alcohol while you are on your medication, you can still have impaired reflexes. Ask your doctor about potential side effects from consuming alcohol while on your medication.

Marijuana and Cocaine

Sometimes people with ADD report that the first time they used marijuana or cocaine, their brain finally felt "normal." However, marijuana use has negative side effects such as the loss of short-term memory, lack of motivation, and drowsiness. Cocaine has side effects of agitation, paranoia, and aggression. If you already have ADD, you really can't afford a reduction in short-term memory or mood stability. In addition, you can never be entirely sure what may be mixed in with illegally purchased drugs. Stimulant medication treatment for ADD reduces the chances of cocaine abuse (Levin et al. 2007).

Prescription Medication

In recent years, there has been an increase in the abuse of prescription medication, including OxyContin (oxycodone), Vicodin (hydrocodone/acetaminophen), and Adderall (mixed amphetamine salts immediate-release). About 26 percent of adolescents who are prescribed stimulant medication for ADD sell or give away their medication (Poulin 2007). In a survey of nine thousand college students, 8.1 percent had used stimulant medication without a prescription (McCabe, Teter, and Boyd 2006). It is very important that you take your medication only as prescribed and never sell your medication or give it to someone. If someone died as a result of taking your medication, you could be charged with manslaughter, not to mention receiving a felony charge for dealing or distributing a controlled substance.

Signs of Addiction

If you think you might have a problem with using drugs, it may be helpful to learn what exactly qualifies as being "addicted." When you are dependent on, or addicted to, a substance, you may experience a build-up of tolerance to the drug and you may also experience withdrawal.

- **Tolerance.** When you need more and more of a substance in order to get the same effect from it, you are building up a *tolerance*. For example, one joint isn't getting you high anymore; now you need two or even three to get the same effect. The amount of time it takes your mind and body to build up tolerance depends on the substance that is being abused, the amount you use each time, and how frequently you use it.

- **Withdrawal.** Withdrawal comes in two forms—psychological and physiological. *Withdrawal* happens when you have a psychological (mind) or physiological (body) reaction when you cut back or stop using a substance. You can experience psychological withdrawal symptoms such as aggression, confusion, and paranoia. You can also experience the physiological effects of withdrawal, including nausea, shaking, and seizures.

What to Do If You Think You Are Addicted

If you've realized that your drug or alcohol use is getting out of control, contact your doctor or a mental health professional and tell them about your drug and alcohol use. It is important that you let them know what drug you are using, how much you are using, and how often you use it. Your prescribed medications may interact with your "self-medications." You especially want to talk to your doctor if you are cutting back on your drug use or stopping altogether, due to the possible withdrawal effects. In the case of alcohol, if you are a long-time abuser, stopping abruptly can lead to confusion and even seizures. There are treatment programs available that can help you safely come down from your use. Be honest with yourself and others about your use. Remember, you are not alone—many people with ADD have had issues with addiction.

COMORBID DISORDERS

Comorbid disorders are disorders that a person experiences concurrently. It is very common for people with ADD to have difficulties with depression, anxiety, and even eating disorders as well. It is not clear whether ADD shares some genetic factors with depression and anxiety, if people with ADD are just more prone to depression and anxiety because of the increased difficulties they have experienced, or if the explanation is a combination of genetic and environmental factors.

Depression and Anxiety

Experiencing depression and anxiety is fairly common when you have ADD: about 25 to 50 percent of people with ADD also have difficulties with depression or anxiety (Fischer et al. 2007). Symptoms of depression and anxiety can be very similar and can occur at the same time.

How many of the following possible symptoms of depression and anxiety do you experience? Check off the boxes.

☐ Not enjoying activities like you used to (this is not the same as experiencing boredom)

☐ Having crying spells or feeling teary

☐ Withdrawing from social activities

☐ Having trouble being cheered up

☐ Dreading getting up in the morning

☐ Being easily irritated

☐ Losing or gaining a significant amount of weight

☐ Feeling panicked for no reason (such as in panic disorder)

☐ Fearing going out in public (such as in social phobia or agoraphobia)

☐ Having difficulty sleeping

☐ Becoming increasingly worried

☐ Waking up too early in the morning and not being able to get back to sleep

☐ Pacing or hand wringing

☐ Moving or talking more slowly than normal

☐ Feeling like you would be better off dead or wishing you could disappear

If you checked off two or more of the boxes, read the "Treatment for Depression and Anxiety" section later in this chapter, which describes whom to contact for help. If you checked off the last box on the list and/or you are feeling like ending your life, contact your local crisis center or call the National Suicide Prevention Lifeline ([800] 273-TALK [8255]). You can also call 911. Be aware that if the police, medical personnel, or mental health professionals feel that you are a danger to yourself or others, they may involuntarily hospitalize you. But the alternative, hurting yourself, is far worse.

DEPRESSIVE DISORDERS

Depressive disorders include major depressive disorder, bipolar disorder I, and *dysthymia* (mild depression). Sometimes a milder form of bipolar disorder, called bipolar II, is mistaken for ADD, and vice versa. This is because the *hypomania* (mild mania) in bipolar I and II can be mistaken for the impulsivity and distractibility found in ADD. One difference between bipolar disorder and ADD is that sometimes people with bipolar disorder can stay up for nights on end without needing any rest. In addition, people with bipolar disorder have high highs (mania) and low lows (depression). In ADD, mood swings may occur, but they are usually not as extreme. Medications called *mood stabilizers* are usually prescribed for bipolar disorder, while antidepressants are usually prescribed for major depressive disorder and dysthymia.

People can also have ADD and depression at the same time. As mentioned above, it's not clear whether people with ADD are more genetically predisposed to depression, or if the frustrations and turmoil of having ADD result in depression, or if depression is caused by a combination of these factors. Medication and counseling can help treat depressive disorders.

ANXIETY DISORDERS

Anxiety disorders include generalized anxiety disorder, obsessive-compulsive disorder, social phobia, and panic disorder. People with ADD tend to have more of these anxiety disorders than the general population (Barkley, Murphy, and Fischer 2008). Sometimes people with ADD have developed *social phobia* (extreme shyness) due to constantly being told to stop talking to their classmates, having a bad habit of interrupting, and also making social mistakes. Some people with ADD may experience symptoms of obsessive-compulsive disorder due to trying to compensate for ADD behaviors. If you've left the front door unlocked before, you may now check it a few times before you go to bed, or you may even turn around and drive home to double-check the lock. Antidepressants and *anxiolytics* (anti-anxiety medications) are commonly prescribed for anxiety disorders. Counseling can also help in the treatment of anxiety disorders.

TREATMENT FOR DEPRESSION AND ANXIETY

Treatment is available for depression and anxiety, but it may be difficult for you to summon up the energy to get help. If this is the case, ask family members or friends to make an appointment for you with a mental health clinician and have them take you to your appointment. Counseling and medication can help you start feeling like you are part of life again. Remember, no one needs to feel this way. There is help available—why not take advantage of it?

In severe cases, feelings of depression and anxiety can cause people to feel suicidal. If you have thoughts of hurting yourself or feel that you would be better off dead, call your local crisis center or call the National Suicide Prevention Lifeline ([800] 273-TALK [8255]). You can also call 911. As mentioned above, be aware that if the police, medical personnel, or mental health professionals feel that you are a danger to yourself or others, they may involuntarily hospitalize you. But the alternative, hurting yourself, is far worse.

Eating Disorders

Women with ADD are four times more likely to have an eating disorder, such as bulimia and anorexia, than non-ADD women (Biederman et al. 2007). In fact, one study found that more ADD adults had an eating disorder than any other comorbid disorder (Mattos et al. 2004). When you have bulimia, you make yourself vomit or use laxatives in order to purge yourself after bingeing on a large amount of food. When you have anorexia, you severely restrict your intake of food and calories. If you suspect you may be bulimic or anorexic, make sure you tell your doctor so you can get the treatment you need. Medications such as Wellbutrin (bupropion) are not recommended to people with eating disorders, due to an increased risk of having a seizure.

SUMMARY

If you have ADD, you are more prone to experiencing substance abuse and other comorbid disorders, like depression, anxiety, and eating disorders. In this chapter, you learned the reasons why people with ADD are more likely to have comorbid disorders. You also learned what help is available when you are experiencing these symptoms. In the next chapter, you will learn about changes you can make in your living space and in your personal habits that can help you more effectively cope with ADD.

CHAPTER 6

LIFESTYLE CHANGES

In chapter 5, you learned about the comorbid disorders of ADD, like substance abuse, depression, anxiety, and eating disorders. Now that you have been diagnosed with ADD, you may be realizing why you are prone to being disorganized and overworked and to having difficulties sleeping. In this chapter, you will learn how to change your living and working environment and practice good self-care so you can cope more effectively with ADD. Good self-care means you get enough sleep and exercise and you make healthy food choices. Change can be a daunting task when you have ADD, but even small changes in your life can make a big difference.

REDUCE CLUTTER AND GET ORGANIZED

It may be difficult to precisely define clutter, but you know it when you see it. You may have items just taking up space on your desk—items you never use. You may have receipts all over the floor of your home office because you do not know if you need them and you don't know how to file them. Clutter creates *visual stress*—a feeling of being overwhelmed because you have too much "stuff" in your environment. Clutter in your home or work environment can sap your energy, leading to inefficiency and a lack of productivity.

PRACTICE EFFECTIVE ORGANIZING

There are ways to create a cleaner living and working environment, including pacing yourself when organizing, using the right organizational tools, and getting someone to help you complete some tasks.

Because people with ADD tend to hyperfocus on projects (even to the point of burnout), set a timer for thirty minutes when you start organizing. Stop when the timer goes off. Take a break for fifteen minutes. Take a walk outside and change the pace of what you are doing. After your break, work for another thirty minutes. Remember to reward yourself for a job well done.

Many people with ADD feel that they cannot have guests over because of the amount of clutter and messiness in their homes. This is unfortunate, because it is so important for people with ADD to have social contact. One short-term solution that can help is to get a large basket or a bin with a lid. If someone is coming over on short notice, take the clutter off your counters and toss it into this container. With the lid on top, no one will ever notice what is inside. You'll have clean counters in no time! Another nice feature about putting clutter in a bin or basket is that you'll have everything in one place when you are ready to sort through it. You'll probably find you didn't really need anything in this container anyway!

Another way to keep organized is by getting a file cabinet with hanging file folders—the large folders in which you can keep several smaller file folders. Label each hanging file folder with the name of a particular category, like "Loans," "Auto," "School," or "Taxes." A hanging folder marked "Loans" would have smaller file folders labeled "Student Loan," "Car Loan," or "Business Loan," for example. You can even color-code these hanging folders—putting your financial papers in a green folder and your legal papers in a blue folder, for example. That way you can open a file drawer and know immediately which hanging file folder you should reach for. People with ADD usually pick up well on visual cues, so color-coding things really helps.

Using a label maker can also be helpful. Store items in clear plastic bins and put a label on each side of each bin saying what is inside each bin. By labeling each side, you'll know for sure what is in the bin, regardless of which way it is stored on the shelf or in the closet. There are digital label makers that are available for a low price. For more information on label makers, see Resources at the end of this book.

Another technique for effective organization is to get an "organization buddy." An organization buddy is a friend, relative, or coworker who assists you while you sort through papers, pay bills, or complete any other organizational task. You want an organization buddy who is organized, patient, understanding, and accepting of ADD. Organization buddies can help you sort through papers, clean out closets, or do any similar task that requires time and detail work. Sometimes just having your organization buddy in the room can help you focus on a task.

If you can't find a friend or relative who would be a good organization buddy, professional organizers can help. Make sure they have an understanding of the chronic disorganization that is a part of ADD. Ask them if they have worked with ADD clients before, and get references.

PRACTICE GOOD SELF-CARE

When you have ADD, you may not be aware of or pay attention to how your body is feeling. This is because people with ADD can get so overwhelmed with the world outside that they don't pay attention to what is going on in their internal world. It is important to take care of yourself by taking breaks, getting enough sleep, exercising, and eating well.

You may have gone hours without eating because you were hyperfocused on a project and did not feel hunger pangs. You may have gone for a while without adequate rest because you were trying to finish an overdue assignment. You may have gained weight because you tend to eat when you are bored and you eat too quickly.

Become Aware of Your Body's Signals

Many times, people with ADD have difficulty picking up on the cues the body is giving them. You may notice some sensations more than others—for example, you can tell when your heart is racing—but when you are distracted, you may not feel your stomach growling. When you become more aware of your body's signals, you can take steps to prevent wearing yourself out. Check in with yourself during the day and ask, "What is my body telling me?" Think about how your body reacts to different situations: with fatigue, hunger, sadness, boredom, or stress. Then figure out a way to take care of that issue. For example, when you are hungry, your stomach may growl, you may feel lightheaded, and your hands may become shaky. To prevent this from happening, make sure you eat every four hours. Carry a snack with you and also keep some snacks in your car and in your desk drawer at work. When you are tired, your eyes may start burning, you may get a headache, and your attention may drift more than usual. Try to get a nap if you can and to get more rest at night. Practicing prevention can make a big difference in your quality of life, and it can help decrease mood swings and irritability.

Take Breaks

When you are doing something you really enjoy, you may hyperfocus or have laser-sharp attention. You may forget to eat or even to go to the bathroom. It is important that you take breaks, even if your brain wants to keep going. Set a timer for thirty minutes, then take a fifteen-minute break, and repeat. During your breaks, get up and move around. One of the best things you can do is go outside for a change of scenery and some fresh air.

Taking a break also means giving yourself a break. Remember, there is only so much in life that you have control over. It is also important to forgive yourself for any past difficulties or mistakes you may have made. You now have a new beginning ahead of you.

Practice Good Sleep Habits

Sleep is your body's built-in healer. If you don't get enough of it, it can be even more difficult for you to focus and keep your emotions in check. If you have ADD, you may have had sleep difficulties since childhood and not even know what it is like to get a good night's rest (Gruber et al. 2008). People with ADD tend to have more problems with insomnia, have more difficulties falling asleep, and have a delayed onset of a brain chemical called melatonin that regulates the body's sleep–wake cycle (Van Veen et al. 2010). If insomnia is a problem for you, seek an evaluation from your doctor or a sleep specialist. Medications, supplements, stress-reduction techniques, and exercise may help you get enough sleep.

Try to get at least eight hours of sleep a night. At least an hour before you go to bed, start to unwind by turning off the television and computer. Electronics can keep the ADD brain jazzed up, so it is best to just turn them off. Switch to a relaxing activity, like reading a book or listening to soothing music. This will help you unwind and get into sleep mode. Having a relaxing environment can really help you get a good night's rest. Invest in some earplugs, keep your bedroom dark, and ban the television from your bedroom.

KNOW YOUR BODY CLOCK

Many people with ADD are night owls—they prefer to be awake during night hours and to sleep during the day. If you are a night owl, it is best to find a career that fits these hours. If this is not possible, try to find a career where you have flexible work hours, so you can arrive later in the morning.

In order to stay on a steady "clock," try to get up every day as close to your usual waking time as possible, even on weekends. The more you can stick to your usual waking time, the easier it will be to adjust when Monday rolls around.

SLEEP DISORDERS

In addition to insomnia, people with ADD tend to have difficulty with teeth grinding and sleep apnea. Some people with ADD grind their teeth (*bruxism*) while they are sleeping or when they are stressed or focusing. If bruxism goes untreated, it can lead to broken, worn down, or sensitive teeth. It can also result in jaw muscle pain and headaches. If you tend to grind your teeth, you can have your dentist fit you for a mouth guard that you wear at night.

Sleep apnea is a serious sleep disorder that can result in even more problems paying attention than usual (Beebe et al. 2004). During a sleep apnea episode, your airway becomes blocked by the soft tissue in the back of your throat. Some people completely stop breathing (in which case we call it apnea) for many seconds, and others have moments where their oxygen levels are so low that their quality of sleep is significantly compromised (which we call hypopnea). Common symptoms of sleep apnea include snoring and waking up still feeling fatigued. Even if you do not fully wake up during the night, your brain may still not be getting the sleep it needs. A test in a sleep lab can help determine if you are experiencing sleep apnea—see your doctor for more information. The treatment for sleep apnea is a CPAP (continuous positive airway pressure) device, a breathing appliance you use at night.

Increase Your Amount of Exercise

Exercise not only helps decrease ADD symptoms—it can also help ease feelings of depression and anxiety (Kiluk, Weden, and Culotta 2009). As you read in chapter 1, people with ADD have a low level of the brain chemical dopamine. Exercising can raise your dopamine level, thereby improving your ability to focus. Exercising first thing in the morning can help you get the maximum benefits of this dopamine boost throughout the day. Just exercising for a minimum of thirty minutes a day, three times a week can help you feel more focused and rested overall. Before starting an exercise program, talk to your doctor.

You may be wondering how you are supposed to start exercising if you've never done it before. Here are a few things to keep in mind as you begin:

- It is important that you have a varied exercise plan. Doing the same activity over and over will just bore you.

- Do activities that are within your ability level, even if you tend to jump into things with 150 percent effort. If you've never really exercised before, it's better to start out by walking around the block than to go rock climbing. Overexertion can lead to injury or even accidents.

- A great motivator is finding an exercise partner. You can ask a friend to join you for a walk, and there are also websites where you can find an exercise partner based on your location, ability level, and preferred activities. Knowing that you are meeting a friend at 6 p.m. to go for a walk can do wonders for getting you out and about. For more information on finding an exercise partner, see Resources at the end of this book.

Eat Appropriately

Food is like medicine for the body, so choose your medication wisely. The adage "You are what you eat" really is true. Cut down on your consumption of refined sugars and processed food. Fresh food is best. In addition, practice portion control. This means eating smaller amounts of food. One way to practice portion control is by using a smaller plate; it can help you feel full, even though you are eating less food. Beware of fad diets or diets that tell you that you need to cut out certain food groups completely. Before you start any diet plan, check with your doctor.

People with ADD eat too quickly, which leads to overeating. You may not realize when you are actually "full." A solution to this problem is to practice *mindful eating*. When you are eating, chew slowly and focus solely on the taste of your food. Do not watch TV or read while you are eating—just eat. Also, when you do eat, sit down at a table instead of standing up, and eat off a plate instead of eating something right out of the box. When you sit down at a table and focus solely on your food, you don't need to eat as much in order to feel satisfied and full. In addition, make sure that what you are eating is really something that appeals to you. You are less likely to overeat if you eat what you enjoy in the first place.

SUMMARY

In this chapter, you learned how changing your surroundings and the way you take care of yourself can pay big dividends in your life. Getting an organization buddy can help you reduce clutter and live a less chaotic life. You also learned that people with ADD can have difficulties practicing good self-care. You learned how to listen to what your body needs, which includes taking breaks, getting enough sleep, exercising adequately, and eating healthy foods. In the next chapter, you will learn another important part of self-care—getting support from others. You will also learn how to talk to your loved ones about having ADD and how to cope when you feel you are not getting the support you need.

CHAPTER 7

GETTING SUPPORT

Now that you have been diagnosed with ADD, you may be searching for a support system—people who can help you through your journey. In this chapter, you will learn about the support available to you—not just from groups, but also from your family and friends. You will also get suggestions on how to talk to others about your ADD, including what to do if you feel you are not getting the support you need.

SUPPORT GROUPS FOR ADD

Sometimes just meeting people with similar life experiences can make the journey easier. Luckily, there are support groups available where you can meet with other adults who have ADD. There are support groups available for ADD adults and groups for parents of ADD children. Some groups are *psychoeducational*, meaning that they talk about the facts of ADD and discuss resources that are available to you. Psychoeducational groups tend to meet about once a month and are generally free of charge or can be attended for a small fee. A *therapeutic* support group gets more into personal stories and discusses feelings and events in people's lives. Therapeutic support groups can meet up to a couple of times a week, with once a week being the standard. Therapeutic groups may have a per-session fee or a flat fee that you pay at the beginning of the group.

Group Confidentiality

A standard rule of support groups is that the information shared in the group stays in the group. It cannot and should not be shared with others. However, confidentiality cannot be guaranteed, especially with an online group. In addition, online confidentiality can never be guaranteed, regardless of the amount of firewalls and virus protection on either side of the Internet connection.

What Happens in a Support Group?

Psychoeducational groups are usually run by one or two leaders. The leaders' role is to keep the group on topic, provide support to group members, coordinate guest speakers, provide resources for group participants, and take care of the financial and logistical aspects of running the group. At the beginning of each group meeting, the leaders introduce themselves and discuss what is on the agenda for the evening. They may have everyone in the group introduce themselves and say what they would like to gain from attending the group. Then a guest speaker gives a talk on a topic related to ADD, such as new advances in the field. A question-and-answer session may follow. The leader then will ask if there are any other topics that participants would like to discuss, and then the meeting is adjourned.

Therapeutic groups are usually run by one or two mental health clinicians. At the beginning of the group meeting, the leaders may summarize the topics discussed in the last meeting. They also remind everyone in the group that confidentiality must be maintained outside the group. Next, members of the group discuss how things have been for each of them since the last meeting. Other group members and the group leaders provide feedback. The group may focus on the experiences of one member for most of the session, particularly if that member is going through a crisis. The leaders wrap up the meeting by summarizing what was discussed, and members may share insights they have learned from their time in the group. For more information on ADD support groups in your area, look under "ADD Organizations" in Resources at the end of this book.

*Adults with ADD need compassion, validation,
practical information, and tips to success. They can
find all this in a supportive group setting.*

—Lori Burack, MSW, LCSW

Online Forums

In cases where a local support group is not available or accessible, Internet forums can be helpful. When you have just a few minutes here and there, these forums are a great place to check in and get some information and support. Remember— as with anything you share on the Internet, confidentiality can never be guaranteed.

Online forums consist of a dialogue between an *original poster*, who presents a topic or question, and *responders*, who give their opinions and suggestions. Reputable online forums have *moderators* who make sure the forum is being used efficiently and respectfully. Forums are usually available at no charge or in exchange for a low yearly membership fee. For more information on online forums, see Resources at the end of this book.

GETTING SUPPORT FROM FAMILY AND FRIENDS

Part of coping with and getting help for ADD is reaching out to the people most important to you—your family and friends. In this section, you will learn how to talk about ADD with your spouse or partner, children, other family members, and friends. By educating your loved ones about ADD, you open a new door to improved communication and understanding.

In addition to talking with your loved ones, give them this book. Tell them that it will help them better understand what things are like in the "ADD world." Acknowledge to your loved ones that you understand that they get frustrated when you do certain things. Let them know that these events are equally frustrating to you and that you are not trying to upset them. Also refer them to the books and websites that are listed in Resources at the end of this book.

Talking with Your Spouse or Partner

In most cases, you spend more time with your spouse or partner than anyone else in your life. Your spouse or partner may have even originally suggested you be evaluated for ADD. If you obtained the ADD diagnosis on your own or this is the first time you are bringing it up with your spouse or partner, you may be concerned about the reaction you might receive. However, don't be surprised if your spouse or partner is actually relieved that there is a name for the behaviors he or she has noticed.

Because people with ADD may not fully realize the impact of their behaviors on others, it may be helpful for your spouse or partner to attend your medication and counseling sessions with you (Knouse et al. 2005). Maybe your spouse or partner has seen some behaviors in you that you have not been previously aware of. This information could give your doctor what he needs to fine-tune your diagnosis. Talk to your doctor or counselor if you would like to bring your spouse or partner to your appointments.

Talking with Your Children

You may wonder if you should tell your child about your ADD diagnosis. For older children, such as teenagers, it may be very helpful to share that information, including educating them about the genetic basis of ADD. It is especially important to explain to your child that having untreated ADD puts a person at greater risk of developing substance abuse, depression, anxiety, or eating disorders. You may also want to emphasize that getting help for ADD can greatly reduce the chances of these things happening. It is important to emphasize to your child that he should feel free to talk to you any time something is worrying him. Just knowing a parent is available to talk can make a huge difference in a child's life.

You also want to let your children know how important it is to take safety precautions (such as wearing a helmet or fastening a seatbelt) before engaging in certain activities. This is because people, especially children, with ADD are more prone to injury and accidents than people without ADD (Sabuncuoglu 2007; Thompson et al. 2007).

Be aware that anything you tell your child may be shared with others. Be especially cautious discussing your use of medication with your children, particularly if you take stimulant medication. You want to make sure that your medication stays safe and secure. Even if your child may not try to get access to your medication, his friends might.

Talking with Your Friends

To whom you disclose your ADD diagnosis depends largely on the amount of trust you have in a person. You want to be fairly certain that your friend will keep your diagnosis in confidence and that he will listen in a nonjudgmental way. When you disclose that you have ADD, tell your friend that you would like the information to be kept just between the two of you. Be aware, however, that confidentiality cannot be guaranteed. Unfortunately, there is still a stigma surrounding mental health issues, but for the most part, you should find plenty of support.

If you feel uncomfortable telling a friend about the diagnosis of ADD, consider just mentioning some areas that you are needing some support in, such as staying organized and cutting back on the amount of interruptions during a conversation. Tell your friend specifically how he can support you—by just listening to you, taking a walk with you during breaks from tasks, or even just giving you a hug when you need one.

Difficulties Getting Support

What if your spouse or partner, family, or friends do not believe ADD exists, think you have been misdiagnosed, or think you shouldn't be taking medication? Sometimes people become frustrated and upset about things they do not understand. If you have ADD, there is a good chance that the important people in your life do not know about the genetic and biological basis of ADD and the symptoms and behaviors that result. If your family or friends feel you were misdiagnosed, talk to them about it. You may learn more about yourself and how your behavior affects others. Take time to speak calmly about your diagnosis. Provide facts about ADD, such as that ADD is a genetic and biological disorder and that several genes for ADD have been identified. You will get much further in educating others if you keep a calm and steady demeanor.

WORKPLACE SUPPORT

Once you have received a diagnosis of ADD, you may want to consider making or obtaining accommodations in your workplace. *Accommodations* are ways that you or your employer can adjust your work environment to make it easier for you to focus and be efficient at your job. Workplace accommodations include getting all of your employer's instructions in a written format or having an office with a door instead of working in an open cubicle. You can get accommodations by either making

105

adjustments to your work space and work habits on your own or asking your employer for accommodations. The more accommodations you can acquire on your own, the less you will need to disclose your ADD diagnosis to your employer. In chapter 8, you will learn more about workplace accommodations and disclosing your diagnosis to your employer.

MAKING SOCIAL CONNECTIONS

You may find that your social circle changes after you are diagnosed with ADD. You may find that you are just more comfortable with other people who have ADD. People with ADD tend to find each other—you may see someone across the room that is as fidgety as you are and you are drawn to them like a magnet. When you talk with another ADD person, neither of you notices interruptions or quick changes of topic. You feel more like your conversation "flows." You may also feel that people with ADD "get" you in a way that other people just don't. It can be a comforting and empowering feeling: finally, someone understands.

If you'd like to meet more people, try joining organizations, religious groups, or intramural sports teams, or form your own social network by meeting people in your community. Even just by attending an event, you will meet people. The saying "Eighty percent of life is just showing up" is true. By joining groups where people have similar interests, you are more likely to meet lasting friends.

> *I've learned that I deserve a partner who loves and accepts me unconditionally, but I first learned that I deserve my own unconditional love and acceptance as well. I've learned to surround myself with people who treat me respectfully and who are generally uplifting, positive, and encouraging.*
>
> —Elecia

SUMMARY

In this chapter, you learned about what support services are available to you. You can seek support from a psychoeducational or therapeutic support group or an online forum. You learned how to seek support from your family and friends, and you learned about accommodations for your workplace. You learned that even if your family and friends cannot provide support, there are other resources available to you. In the next chapter, you will learn more about workplace accommodations, your rights in the workplace, and ways you can find a job that is best suited to the characteristics of ADD.

CHAPTER 8

ADD AND THE WORKPLACE

Now that you have been diagnosed with ADD, you may be wondering how it affects your job, including your relationships with your boss and coworkers. Should you tell people at the office that you have ADD? Is there anything you can do to make your job more ADD-friendly? In this chapter, you will learn about getting accommodations, the unwritten rules of the workplace, and how to find a job that is best suited to you.

WORKPLACE ACCOMMODATIONS

Accommodations are ways that you can adjust your environment in order to be more productive and efficient at your job. First try to make adjustments to your work space and work habits on your own. If you have tried implementing your own accommodations and still need additional help, consider talking with your employer. Workplace accommodations may be legally enforced through the Americans with Disabilities Act (ADA). This act prohibits discrimination due to a disability (including ADD). However, to be covered under the ADA, you must disclose your disability to your employer. If you have disclosed your diagnosis, asked for reasonable accommodations, and still feel that your employer has not followed the law, first try to work with your employer directly before considering legal action. If you feel that legal recourse is your only option, keep in mind that taking legal action is a long and expensive process. For more information on your rights under ADA, see Resources at the end of this book for ADA contact information.

You can try these accommodations in your workplace:

- Take frequent, short breaks during your workday, where you leave your desk and maybe even go outside for some fresh air.

- Replace fluorescent light bulbs. People with ADD can be more sensitive than others to the distracting buzzing sound of fluorescents.

- Take a walk during your lunch break.

- When scheduling your workday, allow extra time for meetings and other work events so you do not overbook yourself.

- Ask for an office that is relatively free from distractions. An office that is out of the main working area is ideal.

- Avoid working in a cubicle. There are too many unavoidable distractions.

- During meetings, keep your hands busy by doing something quietly, like taking notes. Concentrating your physical energy in this way (a process called *concentrated distraction*) makes it easier for you to focus and stay focused.

- Make sure you receive clear deadlines, and be aware of what is expected from you.

- Break large projects into smaller tasks.

- Have flexible work hours.

- Get assignments, instructions, and requests in writing—keep a "paper trail."

> As much as I love my full-time job as a professional
> in child welfare, if I don't work hard to keep myself
> on task, I often forget what I am supposed to be
> doing. For me, the keys to managing my time
> and staying focused are setting timers for myself
> and writing everything down. I obsessively make
> lists so I always remember what has to be done.
> I try to structure my schedule so that I spend the
> appropriate amount of time doing what needs to be
> done and not too much time on less crucial items.
> Of course I still slip up, or don't follow my own
> rules at times, but in general, it's the best plan I've
> found so far.
>
> —Kelly

LEARN THE UNWRITTEN RULES OF THE WORKPLACE

In every office, there are rules that aren't written in your employee manual. An "unwritten" rule in your workplace might be that new employees sit in the back row during a meeting or that a particular administrative assistant has more influence than her boss over getting things done. You may find that you just don't catch on to these unwritten rules. The ability to figure out how to behave in situations without directly being told is called *sapience*. Sapience means to act with appropriate judgment. People

111

with ADD can have quite a bit of difficulty in this area. Many workplaces have employee manuals, but it helps to know the subtle unspoken rules about how things operate.

You may be asking yourself, "How am I supposed to know that stuff?" To learn these unwritten rules, observe how other people in the office behave. When you are more comfortable in your work environment, you can ask someone "in the know" about how things are done at your office.

DEALING WITH COWORKER/ EMPLOYER HARASSMENT

Just as you have rights when it comes to receiving accommodations for ADD, you also have rights in regard to harassment in the workplace. It is common for people with ADD to feel picked on at work because they just don't fit in. Harassment ranges from little comments or digs made here and there, to outright attempts to sabotage you so you can be terminated from employment. Harassment also includes comments of a sexual nature and/or implying that your job is dependent on sexual favors.

Some light teasing is normal in the workplace, as long as everyone involved is okay with it. However, if you tell a coworker that something they said is hurtful or inappropriate, the teasing or harassment should stop. If that doesn't make the behavior stop, talk to your superiors. Provide documentation of the dates, times, and exact wording of conversations with this coworker or employer, including documentation of how you clearly told this person to stop the harassment. If you are not getting relief from your employer, consider contacting the corporate headquarters of your company or seeking the advice of an attorney. Remember, legal means are a last resort due to the time, energy, and costs involved.

FIND A JOB BEST SUITED TO YOUR NEEDS

Loss of productivity due to ADD costs between $67 billion and $116 billion annually in the United States (Biederman and Faraone 2006). People with ADD are more likely to change jobs and get fired from jobs than their non-ADD peers. They are also more likely to miss days from work than other employees (Birnbaum et al. 2005; Secnik, Swensen, and Lage 2005). These things may happen more often when you have ADD in part because you've had jobs that worked against your ADD instead of working with it.

Jobs that are ADD-friendly tend to have the following characteristics:

- They are fast-paced, with varied tasks each day.

- You can move around or travel during the workday.

- They are intellectually stimulating and challenging.

- There are firm due dates for projects.

- You get frequent feedback, and expectations are clear.

- The schedule is flexible.

- There is immediate reinforcement for a job well done.

For example, work as a firefighter, a restaurant waitperson, a teacher, a paramedic, an emergency room physician, a trial attorney, or a soldier encompasses many of the characteristics of ADD-friendly jobs. Jobs that require repetitive tasks, lack structure, give little feedback, have vague expectations, lack employer support, and have a lot of unwritten rules are more of a challenge. To determine whether your job is ADD-friendly, consider whether it meets the characteristics of other jobs in which people with ADD excel.

In addition to considering the characteristics of a job, consider how well a job meshes with your body clock. Working with your body clock instead of fighting it can make a job ADD-friendly too. In chapter 6, you learned that people with ADD tend to be night owls. If your brain is more awake and alert between the hours of 1 p.m. and 3 a.m., having a job that starts at 8 a.m. may not be the best idea. Fields that allow people to work night hours include health care (e.g., being a nurse, paramedic, or lab worker), protective service (e.g., being a firefighter, police person, or security guard), and food service (e.g., being a baker or pastry chef). You may even be able to work night hours at your current job. Technology has made it possible for people to telecommute at all hours of the day (and night). Talk to your employer about this possibility.

HOW TO FIND THE RIGHT CAREER FOR YOU

Let's say you've decided that you want to find a more ADD-friendly job. However, you may be concerned about leaving the security of your current job. Rest assured that once you find something you are excited about, you will love working at it— and your passion and joy for your work will show, thereby attracting more clients, business, and promotions. If you are trying to find your passion, think back to a time where you enjoyed a task so much that you felt like you were in "the zone," and time just flew by. How can you translate that activity into a career? There are professionals who can help you fine-tune whatever career might be best for you. You can find certified career counselors in private practice, in a career counseling center, or at a vocational rehabilitation center. Career counselors meet with you to learn about your previous work experience, interests, skills, and challenges. They can also give you assessment tests to further pinpoint a recommended career path. These services may be available for free or for an hourly fee, depending on where the career counselor is located. You can find more information on career counselors in Resources at the end of this book.

ENTREPRENEURS

Owning your own business can be both a dream and a nightmare if you have ADD. You love being your own boss—you make the rules and you have more flexibility with your schedule. The good news is that you call all of the shots. The bad news is, well, you call all of the shots. You are now solely responsible for your business's survival. You may be lacking the structure that you used to have when you had an employer: your boss is no longer reminding you to turn in an assignment or assigning you deadlines. And since it is now all up to you, it is very important to have employee support when you have ADD and are running your own business.

Most successful entrepreneurs will tell you that they owe a lot of their success to their great administrative assistants and staff. You may feel like you can't afford to hire employees at this stage of your business. But what you may not realize is that you could actually make more money in the long run if you had someone to help you out. You are an idea person—you just need someone to impose structure and help you carry those ideas through to completion. By having a good support team, you can spend more time doing the things you are good at—which translates into more money and more enjoyment on your part.

SUMMARY

In this chapter, you learned how ADD affects your ability to cope with and function in your job. You found out about workplace accommodations and you learned about your rights under ADA. You discovered which job characteristics best suit a person with ADD and found out how you can get more information on choosing the best career path for you. In the next chapter, you will learn about the positive characteristics of ADD, including being creative, having a good sense of humor, and having a strong sense of justice.

CHAPTER 9

THE POSITIVES OF HAVING ADD

Considering the negative feedback you may have received in the past regarding your impulsive behavior, it might surprise you to learn that there are positives to having ADD. The things that got you in trouble when you were a kid have a flip side to them!

People with ADD can have the following traits:

- Creativity

- Versatility

- Good sense of humor

- Appreciation of nature and the outdoors

- Laser-sharp focus

- Friendliness

- Strong sense of justice

- Empathy

- Persuasiveness

- Zest for life

CREATIVITY

When you were a kid, that blank wall in the family room was just a canvas that needed to be filled. You thought you created a masterpiece with your crayons—your mother felt otherwise. However, now you can channel that creativity in positive ways. You may be artistically gifted, you may be great at coming up with ideas for advertising campaigns, or you may be able to find solutions for what appear to be unsolvable problems. The ADD brain can be a fertile ground for all sorts of ideas. You come up with ideas that other people just don't think of, because your brain works more quickly and you aren't held back by constraints (Abraham et al. 2006).

You may be concerned that taking medication for ADD will result in a dulling of your creative side. Actually, medication can help you channel your creative energy, leading you to produce more work than before (Farah et al. 2009). It works best when you can create wonderful ideas for an organization and other team members help carry those ideas out.

VERSATILITY

When you were a kid, your parents and teachers told you that you jumped around too much from activity to activity. You would leave a tornado of toys in your wake. Now that you are an adult, you may find that you lose people when you switch conversation topics quickly, and you may have a bunch of unfinished projects around the house or at work. However, this ability to "switch tracks" and start new activities has benefits as well. You may excel at jobs where being quick on your feet is a plus. Your brain feels more "on" and alive when you are working at a fast pace.

This may be why people with ADD do well in jobs in high-pressure situations, such as working in an emergency room or being a firefighter. You may also do really well in crisis situations. Your ability to switch tasks easily also means that you have experience in many different areas of life. You can talk to people about quantum physics, cook a soufflé, and design your own web page—all at the same time!

GOOD SENSE OF HUMOR

You were always cracking jokes when you were a kid—you were known as the class clown. You always had your classmates cracking up, even during "quiet time." Your teacher did not take too kindly to this. But you were hilarious. As an adult, your ADD brain still can take twists and turns that help you come up with some naturally funny material.

You may also have no concept of this thing people refer to as "stage fright." You love having an audience. You could give a lecture in front of five hundred people with no problem. And when you give a lecture, you are very good at it. The audience is riveted while you speak. In addition, you have the ability to see humor and absurdity in situations that look hopeless to others. You lighten the mood, and you help everyone put things into perspective. Having a great sense of humor can be an incredible gift you give to others.

APPRECIATION OF NATURE AND THE OUTDOORS

When you were a kid, your mother had to put extra deadbolts on the door—you were always trying to escape so you could play outside. Now that you are an adult, you may find that you love being outside, taking in nature and the world around you. You may feel calmer just by being in the fresh air. In fact, being outside can help reduce the impact of your ADD (Taylor and

Kuo 2009). When you are outdoors, you may feel a connection with nature that others don't experience—you feel like you are part of a bigger plan and that all living things are connected to each other. Your interest may lead to a career in wildlife conservation or forestry.

Being outside, for me, is not a luxury—it's a necessity. I really can't sit still and focus until I've been outside doing something. It's part of my daily routine, just like brushing my teeth.

—Alicia

LASER-SHARP FOCUS

When you were playing video games when you were a kid, you didn't just play the games—you were *inside* them. Your dad would eventually have to come up and shut off the computer or TV because you just didn't hear him the three times he yelled for you. Now that you are an adult, you may get so into an interesting project that everything just seems to fall away and time flies by. You may think it's strange that one of the features of ADD is that you can actually pay attention really well! It just has to be something that really interests you. In fact, when you get into your *hyperfocusing* mode, you may pay even better attention than people without ADD!

> *When it comes to a few select things I tend to obsess over, I can engage in them for hours at a time uninterrupted. With my freelance photography, I'm completely focused on the session, get incredibly excited over how my images will turn out, and then can spend tons of time sorting through them and editing them without distraction. When I am reading or researching something I am fascinated by, I become completely absorbed and get lost in the material.*
>
> —Kelly

FRIENDLINESS

When you accompanied your mom to the grocery store, you would immediately run off and introduce yourself to random people in the store. Your mother was mortified. Now that you are an adult, you are the first person to approach a new coworker or neighbor. You love meeting new people. You have the ability to strike up a conversation anywhere with anyone. Sure, you may not always say the "right" thing, but you've met a lot of interesting people!

You have a natural charisma. People just seem drawn to you. You believe that people are essentially good. It can be difficult for you to comprehend why people would treat others unfairly.

This leads to you having a strong sense of justice, another positive trait of ADD.

You don't hold grudges. In fact, you may give people a shot again and again. You may let anger or upset toward others go away easily—partially because you tend to see the good in all people and partially because you can't remember what they did to get you upset in the first place. You've already moved on to other things!

STRONG SENSE OF JUSTICE

When you were a kid, you would argue your point until the bitter end—even if it resulted in a longer time-out experience. When you're an adult, this can translate into having a strong sense of justice—a clear understanding of right and wrong. You have experienced what it is like to be the outsider or the kid who just didn't fit in, and you are sensitive to how others are treated.

You may root for the underdog or stick up for the person who seems to have an outside shot rather than cheer for the favored winner. When you see injustice done to someone or something, you get angry or fired up. Now you can channel this energy into something positive: You can use that energy to be a catalyst for change. If you get upset about a news story on animal abuse, you can volunteer with an animal protection organization. If you get upset because you don't feel ADD kids are being treated fairly at school, you can get involved with a national ADD organization. You can find more information on ADD organizations in Resources at the end of this book.

EMPATHY

When you were a kid, you may have been more quick to tears than other kids, especially when you were teased. Now you are the one that all your friends go to when they need advice or a shoulder to cry on. You find it easy to understand what others are going through, to the point where you may actually start feeling the same way that they do. You are good at "reading" people—you instantly know if they are good or if you can trust them. You also intuitively know what other people need. You just seem to know the exact right time to call a friend and you know just the right thing to say to help someone feel better.

You are also empathic with animals. When you were a kid, you were always bringing a stray animal home—cats, dogs, birds—whatever animal needed your help. They seem to gravitate toward you, and you naturally seem to know what they need. People tell you that you seem to have a natural knack with other living things. You seem to be able to "listen" to animals.

PERSUASIVENESS

When you were a kid, you would try to negotiate the terms of your punishments with your parents—and sometimes you were able to get your "sentence" reduced or even commuted. Your parents said you would make a great attorney. You also had a knack for talking kids into things—which resulted in some interesting adventures. Now that you are an adult, being persuasive can translate into a successful career in sales, management, international diplomacy, or trial law. You know what a client needs, sometimes without even having to ask them—and you find a way to fill that need. You know how to argue your case swiftly and effectively, and you tailor your message based on who is receiving it. It's almost as if people are hypnotized by you as you speak.

ZEST FOR LIFE

When you were a kid, you didn't have an "off" switch. Your parents said that you didn't really sleep at night—you just recharged. As an adult, you may love waking up in the morning because of all the opportunities that await you. You tend to see the good in every situation, even when things look bleak to others. You are always open to new experiences. People tell you that you "always have your hat on"—you are ready for a new adventure at a moment's notice. You may even inspire people to try new things. The best place for you to travel is a place you've never been before. You are perfectly okay traveling solo. In fact, you may prefer it because then you can see as many things as possible. You live your life without fear.

The good thing about having ADD is that I'm never bored!

—John

SUMMARY

In this chapter, you learned that while you may have received criticism in the past for your ADD behaviors, the flip side is that there are a lot of good things that go along with having ADD. People with ADD can be creative, be versatile, have a good sense of humor, have an appreciation of nature and the outdoors, be sharply focused, be friendly, have a strong sense of justice, be empathic, be persuasive, and have a zest for life. You learned that you can make the world a better place by using these gifts.

CONCLUSION

In this book, you have learned how to have a happier and more productive life with ADD. You learned about what causes ADD. You learned how to find a professional who can best help you. You also discovered the process of ADD evaluations and diagnosis. You learned about treatment options, such as medication, counseling, and coaching. You found out about the comorbid disorders of ADD—substance abuse, depression, anxiety, and eating disorders. You learned about changes you can make in your living environment and in your personal health so you can be more efficient and productive. You also discovered the ways that you can seek support for ADD—both from groups and from your loved ones. You found out about workplace accommodations, your rights under ADA, and how to find a career that is best suited to your skills. You have gained a lot of knowledge for your new adventure with ADD! May you continue to grow and prosper in the future.

·······

RESOURCES

ADD Catalog
ADD WareHouse
addwarehouse.com
(800) 233-9273

ADD Information and Support
ADDvance
addvance.com

ADD Magazines

ADDitude magazine
additudemag.com

Attention magazine
chadd.org

ADD Online Forums

Attention Deficit Hyperactivity Disorder Forums
addforums.com

Living with ADD
livingwithadd.com/forum

ADD Organizations

Attention Deficit Disorder Association (ADDA)
add.org

Children and Adults with Attention Deficit/Hyperactivity
  Disorder (CHADD)
chadd.org

Career Counselors

National Career Development Association
ncda.org

Career Information

U.S. Department of Labor, Bureau of Labor Statistics.
  Occupational Outlook Handbook.
bls.gov/oco

Coaching

ADD Consults
Referral source for counselors and coaches who specialize in
  ADD
addconsults.com

ADHD Coaches Organization
adhdcoaches.org

American Coaching Association
americoach.org
2141 Birch Drive
Lafayette Hill, PA 19444
Phone: (610) 825-8572
Fax: (610) 825-4505

Counselors and Therapists

ADD Referral
addreferral.com

American Counseling Association
counseling.org

American Psychological Association
apa.org

The Family and Marriage Counseling Directory
family-marriage-counseling.com

TherapistLocator.net

The American Association for Marriage and Family Therapy
therapistlocator.net

Depression and Anxiety
Anxiety Disorders Association of America
adaa.org

Depression and Bipolar Support Alliance
dbsalliance.org

Eating Disorders
National Eating Disorders Association
edap.org

Exercise Partners
Exercise Friends
exercisefriends.com

Find an Exercise Partner
findanexercisepartner.com

Insurance Claims Clearinghouse
Medical Information Bureau (MIB Group Inc.)
mib.com
For MIB record information: (866) 692-6901

Label Makers
Brother
brother.com

DYMO
dymo.com

Medication
National Resource Center on AD/HD. "Medication
  Management for Adults with ADHD."
addresources.org/article_adhd_medication_chadd.php

National Alliance on Mental Illness
nami.org

Note that the following websites are those of pharmaceutical
  companies:

Concerta (methylphenidate HCl extended-release)
concerta.net

Daytrana (methylphenidate transdermal)
daytrana.com

Intuniv (guanfacine extended-release)
intuniv.com

Strattera (atomoxetine)
strattera.com

Vyvanse (lisdexamfetamine)
vyvanse.com

Professional Organizers

National Association of Professional Organizers
napo.net
15000 Commerce Parkway
Suite C
Mount Laurel, NJ 08054
Phone: (856) 380-6828
Fax: (856) 439-0525

Professional Organizers Online
professionalorganizersonline.com

Suicide Prevention

National Suicide Prevention Lifeline
(800) 273-TALK (8255)

U.S. nationwide emergency telephone number: 911

Workplace Rights

Americans with Disabilities Act (ADA)
U.S. Department of Justice
ada.gov
ADA Information Line:
Phone: (800) 514-0301
TTY: (800) 514-0383

·······

RECOMMENDED READING

Albrecht, A. T. 2010. *100 Questions & Answers About Adult ADHD*. Boston: Jones & Bartlett Publishers.

Hallowell, E. M., and J. J. Ratey. 1995. *Driven to Distraction: Recognizing and Coping with Attention Deficit Disorder from Childhood Through Adulthood*. New York: Touchstone.

———. 2005. *Delivered from Distraction: Getting the Most Out of Life with Attention Deficit Disorder*. New York: Ballantine Books.

———. 2010. *Answers to Distraction*. New York: Anchor Books.

Honos-Webb, L. 2008. *The Gift of Adult ADD: How to Transform Your Challenges & Build on Your Strengths*. Oakland, CA: New Harbinger Publications.

Kelly, K., and P. Ramundo. 2006. *You Mean I'm Not Lazy, Stupid or Crazy?!: The Classic Self-Help Book for Adults with Attention Deficit Disorder.* New York: Scribner.

Kolberg, J. 1998. *Conquering Chronic Disorganization.* Decatur, GA: Squall Press.

Kolberg, J., and K. Nadeau. 2002. *ADD-Friendly Ways to Organize Your Life.* New York: Routledge.

Novotni, M. 1999. *What Does Everybody Else Know That I Don't?: Social Skills Help for Adults with Attention Deficit/Hyperactivity Disorder (AD/HD).* Plantation, FL: Specialty Press.

Pera, G. 2008. *Is It You, Me, or Adult A.D.D.?: Stopping the Roller Coaster When Someone You Love Has Attention Deficit Disorder.* San Francisco: 1201 Alarm Press.

Ratey, N. A. 2008. *The Disorganized Mind: Coaching Your ADHD Brain to Take Control of Your Time, Tasks, and Talents.* New York: St. Martin's Press.

Sarkis, S. 2006. *10 Simple Solutions to Adult ADD: How to Overcome Chronic Distraction & Accomplish Your Goals.* Oakland, CA: New Harbinger Publications.

———. 2008. *Making the Grade with ADD: A Student's Guide to Succeeding in College with Attention Deficit Disorder.* Oakland, CA: New Harbinger Publications.

Sarkis, S., and K. Klein. 2009. *ADD and Your Money: A Guide to Personal Finance for Adults with Attention-Deficit Disorder.* Oakland, CA: New Harbinger Publications.

Tuckman, A. 2009. *More Attention, Less Deficit: Success Strategies for Adults with ADHD.* Plantation, FL: Specialty Press.

Weiss, L. 2005. *Attention Deficit Disorder in Adults: A Different Way of Thinking* (Revised 4th ed.). New York: Taylor Trade Publishing.

········

REFERENCES

Abraham, A., S. Windmann, R. Siefen, I. Daum, and O. Güntürkün. 2006. Creative thinking in adolescents with attention deficit hyperactivity disorder (ADHD). *Child Neuropsychology* 12(2):111–123.

Antalis, C. J., L. J. Stevens, M. Campbell, R. Pazdro, K. Ericson, and J. R. Burgess. 2006. Omega-3 fatty acid status in attention-deficit/hyperactivity disorder. *Prostaglandins, Leukotrienes and Essential Fatty Acids* 75(4–5):299–308.

Antshel, K. M., S. V. Faraone, K. Maglione, A. E. Doyle, R. Fried, L. J. Seidman, and J. Biederman. 2010. Executive functioning in high-IQ adults with ADD. *Psychological Medicine*. Published online by Cambridge University Press, January 20, http://journals.cambridge.org/action/displayAbstract?aid=7096464.

APA (American Psychiatric Association). 1968. *Diagnostic and Statistical Manual of Mental Disorders* (2nd ed.). Washington, DC: Author.

————. 1980. *Diagnostic and Statistical Manual of Mental Disorders* (3rd ed.). Washington, DC: Author.

————. 1987. *Diagnostic and Statistical Manual of Mental Disorders* (Revised 3rd ed.). Washington, DC: Author.

————. 1994. *Diagnostic and Statistical Manual of Mental Disorders* (4th ed.). Washington, DC: Author.

————. 2000. *Diagnostic and Statistical Manual of Mental Disorders* (Revised 4th ed.). Washington, DC: Author.

Barkley, R. A. 2005. *Attention-Deficit Hyperactivity Disorder: A Handbook for Diagnosis and Treatment.* 3rd ed. New York: The Guilford Press.

Barkley, R. A., M. Fischer, L. Smallish, and K. Fletcher. 2005. Young adult outcome of hyperactive children: Adaptive functioning in major life activities. *Journal of the American Academy of Child and Adolescent Psychiatry* 45(2):192–202.

Barkley, R. A., and K. R. Murphy. 1998. *Attention-Deficit Hyperactivity Disorder: A Clinical Workbook.* New York: The Guilford Press.

Barkley, R. A., K. R. Murphy, and M. Fischer. 2008. *ADHD in Adults: What the Science Says.* New York: The Guilford Press.

Beebe, D. W., C. T. Wells, J. Jeffries, B. Chini, M. Kalra, and R. Amin. 2004. Neuropsychological effects of pediatric obstructive sleep apnea. *Journal of the International Neuropsychological Society* 10(7):962–975.

Bernfort, L., S. Nordfeldt, and J. Persson. 2008. ADD from a socio-economic perspective. *Acta Paediatrica* 97(2):239–245.

Biederman, J. 2003. Pharmacotherapy for attention-deficit/hyper-activity disorder (ADHD) decreases the risk for substance abuse: Findings from a longitudinal follow-up of youths with and without ADHD. *Journal of Clinical Psychiatry* 64(Suppl. 11):3–8.

Biederman, J., S. W. Ball, M. C. Monuteaux, C. B. Surman, J. L. Johnson, and S. Zeitlin. 2007. Are girls with ADHD at risk for eating disorders? Results from a controlled, five-year prospective study. *Journal of Developmental and Behavioral Pediatrics* 28(4):302–307.

Biederman, J. and S. V. Faraone. 2006. The effects of attention-deficit/hyperactivity disorder on employment and household income. *Medscape General Medicine* 8(3):12.

Biederman J., R. D. Melmed, A. Patel, K. McBurnett, J. Konow, A. Lyne, and N. Scherer, for the SPD503 Study Group. 2008. A randomized, double-blind, placebo-controlled study of guanfacine extended release in children and adolescents with attention-deficit/hyperactivity disorder. *Pediatrics* 121(1):e73–e84.

Biederman, J., M. C. Monuteaux, E. Mick, T. E. Wilens, J. A. Fontanella, K. M. Poetzl, T. Kirk, J. Masse, and S. V. Faraone. 2006. Is cigarette smoking a gateway to alcohol and illicit drug use disorders?: A study of youths with and without attention deficit hyperactivity disorder. *Biological Psychiatry* 59(3):258–264.

Biederman, J., M. C. Monuteaux, T. Spencer, T. E. Wilens, and S. V. Faraone. 2009. Do stimulants protect against psychiatric disorders in youth with ADHD? A 10-year follow-up study. *Pediatrics* 124(1):71–78.

Biederman, J., M. C. Monuteaux, T. Spencer, T. E. Wilens, H. A. MacPherson, and S. V. Faraone. 2008. Stimulant therapy and risk for subsequent substance use disorders in male adults with ADHD: A naturalistic controlled 10-year follow-up study. *American Journal of Psychiatry* 165(5):597–603.

Birnbaum, H. G., R. C. Kessler, S. W. Lowe, K. Secnik, P. E. Greenbaum, S. A. Leong, and A. R. Swensen. 2005. Costs of attention deficit-hyperactivity disorder (ADHD) in the U. S.: Excess costs of persons with ADHD and their family members in 2000. *Current Medical Research and Opinion* 21(2):195–206.

Breyer, J., A. Botzet, K. Winters, R. Stinchfield, and G. August. 2009. Young adult gambling behaviors and their relationship with the persistence of ADD. *Journal of Gambling Studies* 25(2):227–238.

Brown, T. E. 1996. *Brown Attention-Deficit Disorder Scales*. San Antonio, TX: Psychological Corporation.

———. 2009. ADD/ADD and impaired executive function in clinical practice. *Current Attention Disorders Reports* 1(1):37–41.

Carmody, T. P., C. Duncan, J. A. Simon, S. Solkowitz, J. Huggins, S. Lee, and K. Delucchi. 2008. Hypnosis for smoking cessation: A randomized trial. *Nicotine & Tobacco Research* 10(5):811–818.

Culbertson, W. C., and E. A. Zillmer. 1999. *Tower of London: Examiner's Manual*. North Towanda, NY: Multi-Health Systems Inc.

Curtis, P., and S. Gaylord. 2005. Safety issues in the interaction of conventional, complementary, and alternative health care. *Complementary Health Practice Review* 10(1):3–31.

DuPaul, G. J., T. J. Power, A. D. Anastopoulos, and R. Reid. 1998. *ADHD Rating Scale-IV: Checklists, Norms, and Clinical Interpretation*. New York: The Guilford Press.

Elia, J., X. Gai, H. M. Xie, J. C. Perin, E. Geiger, J. T. Glessner, et al. 2010. Rare structural variants found in attention-deficit hyperactivity disorder are preferentially associated with neurodevelopmental genes. *Molecular Psychiatry* 15(6):637–646.

Farah, M. J., C. Haimm, G. Sankoorikal, and A. Chatterjee. 2009. When we enhance cognition with Adderall, do we sacrifice creativity? A preliminary study. *Psychopharmacology* 202(1):541–547.

Fischer, M., R. A. Barkley, L. Smallish, and K. Fletcher. 2007. Hyperactive children as young adults: Driving abilities, safe driving behavior, and adverse driving outcomes. *Accident Analysis and Prevention* 39(1):94–105.

Flory, K., B. S. Molina, W. E. Pelham, E. Gnagy, and B. Smith. 2006. Childhood ADD predicts risky sexual behavior in young adulthood. *Journal of Clinical Child and Adolescent Psychology* 35(4):571–577.

Foti, F. S., J. L. Wahlstrom, and L. C. Wienkers. 2007. The in vitro drug interaction potential of dietary supplements containing multiple herbal components. *Drug Metabolism & Disposition* 35(2):185–188.

Frankos, V. H., D. A. Street, and R. K. O'Neill. 2010. FDA regulation of dietary supplements and requirements regarding adverse event reporting. *Clinical Pharmacology & Therapeutics* 87(2): 239–244.

Gehricke, J., C. Whalen, L. Jamner, T. Wigal, and K. Steinhoff. 2006. The reinforcing effects of nicotine and stimulant medication in the everyday lives of adult smokers with ADHD: A preliminary examination. *Nicotine & Tobacco Research* 8(1):37–47.

Gevensleben, H., B. Holl, B. Albrecht, C. Vogel, D. Schlamp, O. Kratz, P. Studer, A. Rothenberger, G. H. Moll, and H. Heinrich. 2009. Is neurofeedback an efficacious treatment for ADHD? A randomised controlled clinical trial. *Journal of Child Psychology and Psychiatry* 50(7):780–789.

Gruber, R., T. Xi, S. Frenette, M. Robert, P. Vannasinh, and J. Carrier. 2008. Sleep disturbances in prepubertal children with attention deficit hyperactivity disorder: A home polysomnography study. *Sleep* 32(3):343–350.

Guan, L., B. Wang, Y. Chen, L. Yang, J. Li, and Q. Qian. 2009. A high-density single-nucleotide polymorphism screen of 23 candidate genes in attention deficit hyperactivity disorder: Suggesting multiple susceptibility genes among Chinese Han population. *Molecular Psychiatry* 14(5):546–554.

Halmey, A., O. B. Fasmer, C. Gillberg, and J. Haavik. 2009. Occupational outcome in adult ADD: Impact of symptom profile, comorbid psychiatric problems, and treatment. *Journal of Attention Disorders* 13(2):175–187.

Hammerness, P., R. Doyle, M. Kotarski, A. Georgiopoulos, G. Joshi, S. Zeitlin, and J. Biederman. 2009. Atomoxetine in children with attention-deficit hyperactivity disorder with prior stimulant therapy: A prospective open-label study. *European Child & Adolescent Psychiatry* 18(8):493–498.

143

Haskard Zolnierek, K. B., and M. R. DiMatteo. 2009. Physician communication and patient adherence to treatment: A meta-analysis. *Medical Care* 47(8):826–834.

Izzo, A. A., and E. Ernst. 2009. Interactions between herbal medicines and prescribed drugs: An updated systematic review. *Drugs* 69(13): 1777–1798.

Jensen, P. 2009. Methylphenidate and psychosocial treatments either alone or in combination reduce ADHD symptoms. *Evidence-Based Mental Health* 12(1):18.

Kessler, R. C., L. Adler, M. Ames, O. Demler, S. Faraone, E. Hiripi, et al. 2005. The World Health Organization adult ADHD self-report scale (ASRS): A short screening scale for use in the general population. *Psychological Medicine* 35(2):245–256.

Kieling, C., R. R. Kieling, L. A. Rohde, P. J. Frick, T. Moffitt, J. T. Nigg, R. Tannock, and F. X. Castellanos. 2010. The age at onset of attention deficit hyperactivity disorder. *American Journal of Psychiatry* 167(1):14–16.

Kiluk, B. D., S. Weden, and V. Culotta. 2009. Sport participation and anxiety in children with ADHD. *Journal of Attention Disorders* 12(6):499–506.

Kleinman, N. L., M. Durkin, A. Melkonian, and K. Markosyan. 2009. Incremental employee health benefit costs, absence days, and turnover among employees with ADD and among employees with children with ADD. *Journal of Occupational and Environmental Medicine* 51(11):1247–1255.

Knouse, L. E., C. L. Bagwell, R. A. Barkley, and K. R. Murphy. 2005. Accuracy of self-evaluation in adults with ADHD: Evidence from a driving study. *Journal of Attention Disorders* 8(4):221–234.

Kollins, S. H., F. J. McClernon, and B. F. Fuemmeler. 2005. Association between smoking and attention-deficit/hyperactivity disorder symptoms in a population-based sample of young adults. *Archives of General Psychiatry* 62(10):1142–1147.

Levin, J. R., S. M. Evans, D. J. Brooks, and F. Garawi. 2007. Treatment of cocaine dependent treatment seekers with adult ADHD: Double-blind comparison of methylphenidate and placebo. *Drug and Alcohol Dependence* 87(1):20–29.

Lindsay, S. E., G. A. Gudelsky, and P. C. Heaton. 2006. Use of modafinil for the treatment of attention deficit/hyperactivity disorder. *Annals of Pharmacotherapy* 40(10):1829–1833.

Mattos, P., E. Saboya, V. Ayrão, D. Segenreich, M. Duchesne, and G. Coutinho. 2004. Comorbid eating disorders in a Brazilian attention-deficit/hyperactivity disorder adult clinical sample. *Revista Brasiliera a de Psiquiatria* 26(4):248–250.

Mazaheri, A., S. Coffey-Corina, G. R. Mangun, E. M. Bekker, A. S. Berry, and B. A. Corbett. 2010. Functional disconnection of frontal cortex and visual cortex in attention-deficit/hyperactivity disorder. *Biological Psychiatry* 67(7):617–623.

McAlonan, G. M., V. Cheung, S. E. Chua, J. Oosterlaan, S. Hung, C. Tang, et al. 2009. Age-related grey matter volume correlates of response inhibition and shifting in attention-deficit hyperactivity disorder. *British Journal of Psychiatry* 194(2):123–129.

McCabe, S., C. Teter, and C. Boyd. 2006. Medical use, illicit use, and diversion of prescription stimulant medication. *Journal of Psychoactive Drugs* 38(1):43–56.

McGough, J. J., J. Biederman, L. L. Greenhill, J. T. McCracken, T. J. Spencer, K. Posner, S. Wigal, J. Gornbein, S. Tulloch, and J. M. Swanson. 2003. Pharmacokinetics of SLI381 (ADDERALL XR), an extended-release formulation of Adderall. *Journal of the American Academy of Child and Adolescent Psychiatry* 42(6): 684–691.

Mitra, A., A. Mitra, D. Pal, M. Minocha, and D. Kwatra. 2010. Compatibility risks between drugs and herbal medicines or botanical supplements. *Toxicology Letters* 196(1): S17.

Newcorn, J. H., C. J. Kratochvil, A. J. Allen, C. D. Casat, D. D. Ruff, R. J. Moore, D. Michelson, and Atomoxetine/Methylphenidate Comparative Study Group. 2008. Atomoxetine and osmotically released methylphenidate for the treatment of attention deficit hyperactivity disorder: Acute comparison and differential response. *American Journal of Psychiatry* 165(6):721–730.

Poulin, C. 2007. From attention-deficit/hyperactivity disorder to medical stimulant use to the diversion of prescribed stimulants to non-medical stimulant use: Connecting the dots. *Addiction* 102(5):740–751.

Quinlan, D. M. 2000. Assessment of attention-deficit/hyperactivity disorder and comorbidities. In *Attention Deficit Disorders and Comorbidities in Children, Adolescents, and Adults*, edited by T. E. Brown. Washington DC: American Psychiatric Association.

Reynolds, C. R. 2002. *Comprehensive Trail-Making Test: Examiner's Manual*. Austin, TX: PRO-ED.

Ribeiro, S. N., C. Jennen-Steinmetz, M. H. Schmidt, and K. Becker. 2008. Nicotine and alcohol use in adolescent psychiatric inpatients: Associations with diagnoses, psychosocial factors, gender and age. *Nordic Journal of Psychiatry* 62(4):315–321.

Rietveld, M. J. H., J. J. Hudziak, M. Bartels, C. E. M. van Beijsterveldt, and D. I. Boomsma. 2004. Heritability of attention problems in children: Longitudinal results from a study of twins, age 3 to 12. *Journal of Child Psychology and Psychiatry* 45(3):577–588.

Rotblatt, M. D. 1999. Herbal medicine: A practical guide to safety and quality assurance. *Western Journal of Medicine* 171(3): 172–175.

Sabuncuoglu, O. 2007. Traumatic dental injuries and attention-deficit/hyperactivity disorder: Is there a link? *Dental Traumatology* 23(3):137–142.

Safren, S. A., P. Duran, I. Yovel, C. A. Perlman, and S. Sprich. 2007. Medication adherence in psychopharmacologically treated adults with ADHD. *Journal of Attention Disorders* 10(3):257–260.

Safren, S. A., M. W. Otto, S. Sprich, C. L. Winett, T. E. Wilens, and J. Biederman. 2005. Cognitive-behavioral therapy for ADHD in medication-treated adults with continued symptoms. *Behaviour Research and Therapy* 43(7):831–842.

Salakari, A., M. Virta, N. Grönroos, E. Chydenius, M. Partinen, R. Vataja, M. Kaski, and M. Iivanainen. 2010. Cognitive-behaviorally-oriented group rehabilitation of adults with ADHD: Results of a 6-month follow-up. *Journal of Attention Disorders* 13(5):516–523.

Sandford, J. A., and A. Turner. 2004. *IVA+Plus™: Integrated Visual and Auditory Continuous Performance Test (IVA+Plus) Administration Manual.* Richmond, VA: BrainTrain.

Sawni, A. 2008. Attention-deficit/hyperactivity disorder and comple-mentary/alternative medicine. *Adolescent Medicine State of the Art Reviews* 19(2):xi, 313–326.

Schuchardt, J. P., M. Huss, M. Stauss-Grabo, and A. Hahn. 2010. Significance of long-chain polyunsaturated fatty acids (PUFAs) for the development and behaviour of children. *European Journal of Pediatrics* 169(2):149–164.

Secnik, K., A. Swensen, and M. J. Lage. 2005. Comorbidities and costs of adult patients diagnosed with attention-deficit hyperactivity dis-order. *Pharmacoeconomics* 23(1):93–102.

Sinn, N., and J. Bryan. 2007. Effect of supplementation with polyun-saturated fatty acids and micronutrients on learning and behavior problems associated with child ADHD. *Journal of Developmental and Behavioral Pediatrics* 28(2):82–91.

Solanto, M. V., D. J. Marks, J. Wasserstein, K. Mitchell, H. Abikoff, J. M. J. Alvir, and M. D. Kofman. 2010. Efficacy of meta-cognitive therapy for adult ADHD. *American Journal of Psychiatry* (advance online publication ahead of print March 15, 2010). DOI (digital object identifier): 10.1176/appi.ajp.2009.09081123.

Solhkhah, R., T. E. Wilens, J. Daly, J. B. Prince, S. L. Van Patten, and J. Biederman. 2005. Bupropion SR for the treatment of substance-abusing outpatient adolescents with attention-deficit/hyperactivity disorder and mood disorders. *Journal of Child and Adolescent Psychopharmacology* 15(5):777–786.

Spencer, T. J. 2009. Issues in the management of patients with complex attention-deficit hyperactivity disorder symptoms. *CNS Drugs* 23(Suppl. 1):9–20.

Still, G. F. 1902. Some abnormal psychical conditions in children. *Lancet* 1:1008–1012.

Taylor, A. F., and F. E. Kuo. 2009. Children with attention deficits concentrate better after walk in the park. *Journal of Attention Disorders* 12(5):402–409.

Teicher, M. 2008. *Quotient™ ADHD System*. Westford, MA: BioBehavioral Diagnostics.

Thompson, A. L., B. S. Molina, W. Pelham, and E. M. Gnagy. 2007. Risky driving in adolescents and young adults with childhood ADD. *Journal of Pediatric Psychology* 32(7):745–759.

Transler, C., A. Eilander, S. Mitchell, and N. van de Meer. 2010. The impact of polyunsaturated fatty acids in reducing child attention deficit and hyperactivity disorders. *Journal of Attention Disorders* (advance online publication ahead of print April 27, 2010). DOI (digital object identifier): 10.1177/1087054709347250.

Trenerry, M., B. Crosson, J. Doboe, and W. Leber. 1989. *Stroop Neuropsychological Screening Test*. Odessa, FL: Psychological Assessment Resources.

Vaughan B., J. Fegert, and C. J. Kratochvil. 2009. Update on atomoxetine in the treatment of attention-deficit/hyperactivity disorder. *Expert Opinion on Pharmacotherapy* 10(4):669–676.

Van Veen, M. M., J. J. S. Kooij, A. N. Boonstra, M. C. M. Gordijn, and E. J. W. Van Someren. 2010. Delayed circadian rhythm in adults with attention-deficit/hyperactivity disorder and chronic sleep-onset insomnia. *Biological Psychiatry* 67(11):1091–1096.

Volkow, N., G. J. Wang, S. H. Kollins, T. L. Wigal, J. H. Newcorn, F. Telang, et al. 2009. Evaluating dopamine reward pathway in ADHD: Clinical implications. *JAMA* 302(10):1084–1091.

Walker, L. R., A. A. Abraham, and K. P. Tercyak. 2010. Adolescent caffeine use, ADHD, and cigarette smoking. *Children's Health Care* 39(1):73–90.

Ward, M. F., P. H. Wender, and F. W. Reimherr. 1993. The Wender Utah Rating Scale: An aid in the retrospective diagnosis of childhood attention deficit hyperactivity disorder. *American Journal of Psychiatry* 150(8):885–890.

Weiss, M., S. A. Safren, M. V. Solanto, L. Hechtman, A. L. Rostain, J. R. Ramsay, and C. Murray. 2008. Research forum on psychological treatment of adults with ADHD. *Journal of Attention Disorders* 11(6):642–651.

Wigal, S. B. 2009. Efficacy and safety limitations of attention-deficit hyperactivity disorder pharmacotherapy in children and adults. *CNS Drugs* 23(Suppl. 1):21–31.

Wilens, T. E. 2004. Attention-deficit/hyperactivity disorder and the substance use disorders: The nature of the relationship, subtypes at risk, and treatment issues. *Psychiatric Clinics of North America* 27(2):283–301.

Wilens, T. E., S. V. Faraone, J. Biederman, and S. Gunawardene. 2003. Does stimulant therapy of attention-deficit/hyperactivity disorder beget later substance abuse? A meta-analytic review of the literature. *Pediatrics* 111(1):179–185.

Wilens, T. E., M. Gignac, A. Swezey, M. C. Monuteaux, and J. Biederman. 2006. Characteristics of adolescents and young adults with ADHD who divert or misuse their prescribed medications. *Journal of the American Academy of Child and Adolescent Psychiatry* 45(4):408–414.

Wilens, T. E., M. C. Monuteaux, L. E. Snyder, H. Moore, J. Whitley, and M. Gignac. 2005. The clinical dilemma of using medications in substance-abusing adolescents and adults with attention-deficit/hyperactivity disorder: What does the literature tell us? *Journal of Child and Adolescent Psychopharmacology* 15(5):787–798.

Wilens, T. E., and H. P. Upadhyaya. 2007. Impact of substance use disorder on ADHD and its treatment. *Journal of Clinical Psychiatry* 68(8):e20.

Yacubian, J., and C. Buchel. 2009. The genetic basis of individual differences in reward processing and the link to addictive behavior and social cognition. *Neuroscience* 164(1):55–71.

Young, G. S., J. A. Conquer, and R. Thomas. 2005. Effect of randomized supplementation with high dose olive, flax or fish oil on serum phospholipid fatty acid levels in adults with attention deficit hyperactivity disorder. *Reproduction, Nutrition, Development* 45(5):549–558.

Stephanie Moulton Sarkis, Ph.D., is adjunct assistant professor at Florida Atlantic University in Boca Raton, FL, and author of *10 Simple Solutions to Adult ADD*, *Making the Grade with ADD*, and *ADD and Your Money*. She is a nationally certified counselor and a licensed mental health counselor, and has a private counseling practice where she specializes in ADD/ADHD counseling and coaching. Sarkis won an American Psychological Association Outstanding Dissertation Award in 2001, and has made media appearances on CNN's *Health Minute*, *Fox News*, *ABC News*, *Sirius Satellite Radio*, *First Business Television*, and numerous other networks and stations. Visit her online at www.stephaniesarkis.com.

Foreword writer **Patricia O. Quinn., MD**, is a developmental pediatrician in Washington, DC. A graduate of Georgetown University Medical School, she specializes in child development and psychopharmacology. She is author of twenty books on attention deficit/hyperactivity disorder for children, adults, and professionals, including the award-winning Attention, Girls!, and cofounded and directs the National Center for Girls and Women with ADHD.

more books from new**harbinger**publications, inc.

Sign up for our Book Alerts at www.newharbinger.com

10 SIMPLE SOLUTIONS TO ADULT ADD

How to Overcome Chronic Distraction and Accomplish Your Goals

US $15.95 / ISBN: 978-1572244344

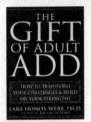

THE GIFT OF ADULT ADD

How to Transform Your Challenges & Build on Your Strengths

US $16.95 / ISBN: 978-1572245655

Also available as an **eBook** at newharbinger.com

BUDDHA'S BRAIN

The Practical Neuroscience of Happiness, Love & Wisdom

US $17.95 / ISBN: 978-1572246959

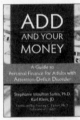

ADD & YOUR MONEY

A Guide to Personal Finance for Adults with Attention-Deficit Disorder

US $18.95 / ISBN: 978-1572247079

STRESS LESS, LIVE MORE

How Acceptance & Commitment Therapy Can Help You Live a Busy yet Balanced Life

US $16.95 / ISBN: 978-1572247093

THE WORRIER'S GUIDE TO OVERCOMING PROCRASTINATION

Breaking Free from the Anxiety That Holds You Back

US $19.95 / ISBN: 978-1572248717

Also available as an **eBook** at newharbinger.com

available from

new**harbinger**publications, inc.

and fine booksellers everywhere

To order, call toll free **1-800-748-6273**
or visit our online bookstore at **www.newharbinger.com**

(VISA, MC, AMEX / prices subject to change without notice)

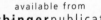

Check out www.psychsolve.com

PsychSolve® offers help with diagnosis, including treatment information on mental health issues, such as depression, bipolar disorder, anxiety, phobias, stress and trauma, relationship problems, eating disorders, chronic pain, and many other disorders.